CRACKING THE COVENANT CODE for kids

KAY ARTHUR
JANNA ARNDT

HARVEST HOUSE PUBLISHERS

All Scripture quotations are taken from the New American Standard Bible®, © 1960, 1962, 1963, 1968, 1971, 1972, 1973, 1975, 1977, 1995 by The Lockman Foundation. Used by permission. (www.Lockman.org)

Illustrations © 2010/2012 by Steve Bjorkman

Cover by Left Coast Design, Portland, Oregon

DISCOVER 4 YOURSELF is a registered trademark of The Hawkins Children's LLC. Harvest House Publishers, Inc., is the exclusive licensee of the federally registered trademark DISCOVER 4 YOURSELF.

CRACKING THE COVENANT CODE FOR KIDS
Copyright © 2012 by Precept Ministries International
Published by Harvest House Publishers
Eugene, Oregon 97402
www.harvesthousepublishers.com

ISBN 978-0-7369-2595-2 (pbk.)
ISBN 978-0-7369-5079-4 (eBook)

Printed in the United States of America

12 13 14 15 16 17 18 19 20 / ML-KBD / 10 9 8 7 6 5 4 3 2 1

HEY, KiDS!

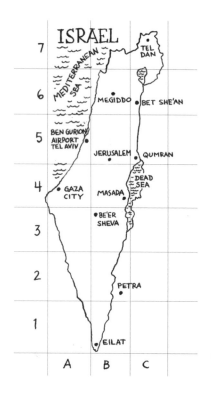

Did you know that Miss Kay and Miss Janna have been to Israel to study the Bible? As you learn about covenant, you're going to discover a lot about the places in Israel Miss Kay and Miss Janna saw and studied. We hope you will love this adventure in Israel. Maybe one day you will get to visit there too!

> Parents, for information about taking a tour to Israel or Precept Ministries, contact Precept Ministries International at 800-763-8280 or visit Precept's website at www.precept.org.

CONTENTS

Uncovering God's Plan—
A Bible Study *You* Can Do!

UNCOVERING GOD'S PLAN—

A BIBLE STUDY YOU CAN DO!

Hey, guys, are you ready to go on a treasure hunt? Molly, Sam (the great face-licking detective beagle), and I have been invited to go to Israel for a treasure hunt with our Uncle Jake, who is an archeologist. By the way, my name is Max. We want you to join us on this great new adventure as we crack secret codes to discover an *amazing* treasure in the Bible called *covenant*. Doesn't that sound exciting?

Did you know that everything God does is based on covenant? *Incredible!* Since covenant is sooooo important to God, we need to find out WHAT covenant is and WHY it's important. WHAT are the different covenants in the Bible? WHO makes a covenant with WHOM? And HOW do these covenants relate to each other?

From reading the Bible, we know that King Saul's son Jonathan and King David were close friends. Jonathan gave David his robe, armor, sword, bow, and belt. In our research, we're going to find out WHY he did that. Did exchanging those things relate to WHAT we are to put on when we enter into covenant with Jesus? HOW do we become followers of Jesus? and WHAT does it cost us to follow Jesus Christ?

We'll get the answers to all these questions by cracking secret codes, using God's Map—the Bible, the source of all truth—and asking the Holy Spirit to lead and guide us.

We also have this book, which is an inductive Bible study.

That word *inductive* means you go straight to the Bible *yourself* to investigate what the Bible shows you about our *awesome* God, our *amazing* Savior, and the blessings of being in covenant with God through Jesus. In inductive Bible study, you "discover 4 yourself" what the Bible says and means.

Aren't you excited? We are! Grab the treasure map God gave us—the Bible—and let's head to Israel for an unbelievable adventure as we crack the covenant code to discover the truth about being in covenant with God and living the life that He has planned for us!

THINGS YOU'LL NEED

New American Standard Bible (Updated Edition, preferably the New Inductive Study Bible— the NISB—Have you gotten yours yet?)

Pen or Pencil

Colored Pencils

Index Cards

A Dictionary

This Workbook

WEEK 1

DISCOVERING THE TREASURE
OF COVENANT

Shalom, it's great to have you in Israel!" Uncle Jake smiled as he hugged Max and Molly at the baggage claim at Ben Gurion Airport.

" 'Shalom,' Uncle Jake?" Max asked.

" 'Shalom' is a Hebrew greeting. It's the way people here say 'hello' and 'good-bye.' It means 'peace,' " Uncle Jake explained.

"Awesome!" Max replied. "Shalom, Uncle Jake."

"Are you guys ready to go on a very special treasure hunt to crack the 'covenant code'?"

"We can't wait!" Max and Molly said at the same time.

"This is going to be so cool," Max said. "We're going on a real treasure hunt in Israel to find out WHAT *covenant* is and WHY it's important."

"And," Molly added, "we get to crack secret codes to help us discover this incredible treasure."

"That's right!" Uncle Jake laughed. "I have quite an adventure planned for you. Let's grab your bags and pick up Sam. 'You know who' is probably going crazy missing you two."

THE ADVENTURE BEGINS

"Sam, pleasssse stop!" Molly giggled as she pushed Sam down when he jumped up to give her a good face-licking.

Uncle Jake laughed. "I told you Sam would be going crazy. Come on, Max. Put Sam on his leash so we can head to the Jeep."

When they got to the Jeep, they all jumped in.

"All right. Are we buckled up and ready to go?" Uncle Jake asked.

"You bet! Where are we going first, Uncle Jake?" Molly asked.

"Look inside the envelope next to you," he said.

Molly opened the envelope and pulled out a treasure map. "Hey, Max, look! It's a treasure map. It has a map of Israel on one side and a map of Jerusalem on the other side."

"That's awesome." Max took a closer look at the map of Israel (on the next page). "Let's see… We are at Ben Gurion Airport in Tel Aviv. By Tel Aviv, there is the word *start* with an arrow pointing to a symbol. That symbol looks like Uncle Jake's special hieroglyphic code. We need to crack this code."

"Uncle Jake, you are so sneaky." Molly smiled as she studied the map. "Max, look inside the guidebook Uncle Jake sent us. I'm sure I saw the key to this code in there."

"You're right, Molly. It's right here (look at page 16). Let me see. Hmmm… I've got it! This symbol stands for the word *Masada*. Our starting point must be Masada."

"That's right, Max." Uncle Jake grinned. "We're on our way to Masada to hunt for God's treasure. Do you remember what we need to do first?"

Molly smiled. "We know!"

How about you, fellow treasure hunter? Do you know what you need to do before you open God's Map (the Bible) to discover priceless treasure? That's right! P__ __ y! Bible study should

TREASURE MAP OF ISRAEL

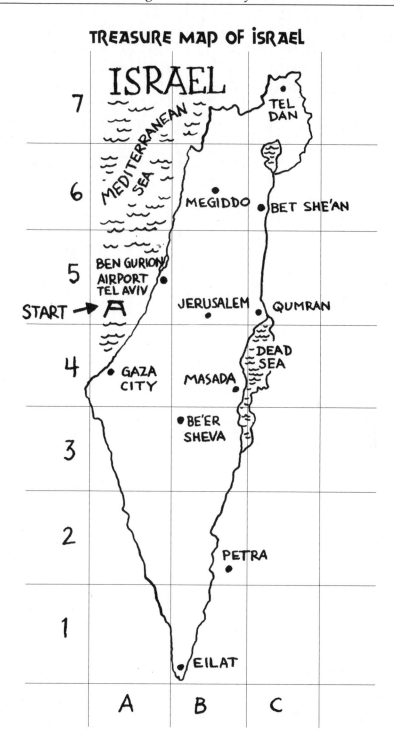

always begin with prayer. We need to ask God to be our Expert Guide on this adventure. We want to ask Him to help us understand what the Bible says and to direct us by His Holy Spirit so we can make sure we understand His Word and handle it accurately.

Let's pray and ask God for His help as we head toward Masada.

Great! Now that you have prayed, take a look at Uncle Jake's field notebook to get some facts about covenant—the treasure we want to uncover in God's Word.

God's Treasure—Covenant

Did you know that everything God does is based on covenant?

Even the Bible is divided into two covenants: the Old Testament and the New Testament. *Testament* is another word for *covenant.*

The Greek word for *covenant* in the New Testament is *diatheke.* It's pronounced *dee-ath-ay'-kay* and means "a contract."

The Hebrew word for *covenant* in the Old Testament is *beriyth.* It's pronounced *ber-eeth'.* It is a "compact" made by passing through pieces of flesh. (We'll discover what this means later. It is a treaty, alliance, pledge, or agreement.

When God makes a covenant it is a lifelong promise that can never be broken.

As you read Uncle Jake's notes, you will notice that he has written down the Greek and Hebrew words for covenant. That's because the original language the Bible was written in was Hebrew with some Aramaic in the Old Testament and Koine Greek in the New Testament. To understand what covenant means, we need to know the original meaning of that word in the Hebrew and Greek languages.

Have you ever made a promise to do something for someone and then broken that promise?

_____ Yes   _____ No

Did you know that when God makes a covenant it is a lifelong promise that will never be broken? That's pretty awesome! Now that we know what covenant is, let's find the *first place* that God uses the word *covenant* in His Word (the Bible). Here is Uncle Jake's first clue to crack the covenant code:

●—→ 6:5-22

To crack this code, turn to page 16 and look for this symbol in Uncle Jake's hieroglyphic code. Write down the word this symbol stands for.

_____

So WHERE will we find the first mention of covenant?

In _____ 6:5-22.

Way to go! One way we can uncover clues as we read God's Map (the Bible) is to look at the people and key words in the passage of Scripture we are studying and mark them in a special way.

Today as we read Genesis 6:5-22, we are going to mark every place we see *God (LORD)* and the word *covenant*. We also need to mark every *pronoun* that refers to God. WHAT are pronouns? Check out Max and Molly's Pronoun Map.

Pronoun Map

Pronouns are words that take the place of nouns. A noun is a person, place, or thing. A pronoun stands in for a noun. Look at the two sentences below. Watch how the pronoun *he* is substituted for Max's name in the second sentence.

> *Max* can't wait to discover the mystery of covenant. *He* wants to know why covenant is so important.

The word *he* is a pronoun because it takes the place of Max's name in the second sentence. *He* is another word we use to refer to Max.

Watch for these other pronouns when you are marking people:

I	you	he	she
me	yours	him	her
mine		his	hers
we	it		
our	its		
they	them		

Now that you know what pronouns are, turn to your Observation Worksheets on page 199. Observation Worksheets have the Bible text printed for you to use as you do this study on covenant.

Read Genesis 6:5-22 and mark every reference to *God* or *LORD* in a special way. You also want to mark *covenant* in a special way just like we have.

God (LORD) (*LORD* is another name that means God) (draw a purple triangle and color it yellow)

covenant (draw a yellow box around it and color it red)

All right! Now that you have marked God's Map, let's find out WHERE covenant is mentioned the very first time in God's Word.

Find the verse where you marked covenant, and write out WHERE you found it on the line below.

Genesis 6:_____

Great work! Now, let's find out WHO makes this first covenant.

Genesis 6:18 WHO makes the covenant?

_____

Genesis 6:18 WHO does this person make a covenant with?

_____

Look what you have discovered! You have just learned that God is the One who established the very first covenant. God makes a covenant with Noah. Remember, when God makes a covenant, it is a promise that can never be broken. This shows us something awesome about God. This shows us God is faithful! We can trust Him to keep His promises. What He says He will do. Isn't that incredible?

So WHAT is this covenant God is making? And WHY is He making it with Noah? We'll find out as we continue to crack the covenant code.

We have one more thing we need to do today before we arrive at Masada. We need to practice our decoding skills by decoding our first memory verse. Each week you will have a new Scripture verse to learn and memorize. This is called "hiding God's Word in your heart."

Decode this week's memory verse by using Uncle Jake's hieroglyphic code below. Find the word in Uncle Jake's hieroglyphic code that matches the symbol in the coded message. Write the word that matches the symbol on the blanks underneath the coded message.

HIEROGLYPHIC CODE

all	and	between	bow	cloud
covenant	creature	earth	everlasting	every
flesh	Genesis	God	I	in
is	it	living	look	of
on	remember	that	the	then
to	upon	when	will	Masada

_____ _____ _____ · _____ _____

_____, _____ _____ _____ _____

_____ _____, _____ _____ _____

_____ _____ _____

_____ _____ _____ _____ _____

_____ _____ _____ _____ · _____

_____ _____. ⟶

_____ 9:16

Fantastic! You did it! Now write your memory verse on an index card. Start memorizing it by reading it out loud three times in a row, three times today.

SEARCHING FOR CLUES

"Wow, Uncle Jake! This is so cool!" Max exclaimed as Uncle Jake stopped the Jeep at the Masada Guest House. "Look at that awesome swimming pool."

Molly grinned. "Do we have time to go swimming, Uncle Jake?"

"We sure do! But first we need to get settled in and prepared for tomorrow's adventure. We have to get up early in the morning to hike up to Masada. It gets really hot up there after the sun comes up."

"Look, Max, there's a envelope on one of the beds!" Molly said when they walked into their room.

"Let's open it," Max said as he sat down on the bed.

Sam jumped up to snatch the envelope.

"Quit, boy! Sit, Sam. It's a clue!" Max declared. "It says, 'To continue your quest, you must go back to the beginning.' "

"I got it!" Molly exclaimed. "Genesis is the first book in the Bible, and yesterday we started our quest in Genesis 6. I bet we need to go back to Genesis 6."

"Good work, Molly," Uncle Jake said. "Okay, you two, let's go to Genesis 6 and uncover more clues about WHY God made the first covenant."

Don't forget to talk to God, treasure hunter! Then grab those colored pencils. Turn to your Observation Worksheets on page 199. Read Genesis 6:5-22, and mark the key people we've listed for you:

man (color it orange)

Noah (and his sons) (color it blue)

Don't forget to mark the pronouns!

Now that you have marked God's Map, let's *contrast* what we learn about *man* in Genesis 6:5-22 to what we learn about Noah. A *contrast* shows how two things are different or opposite, such as *light* and *dark* or *truth* and *lie*.

Look at the following verses and list the words that describe *man* in Genesis 6:5 and *Noah* in Genesis 6:8,9,22. HOW are they different?

Man	**Noah**
Genesis 6:5	Genesis 6:8,9,22
_____	_____
_____	_____
_____	_____
	_____
	_____
	_____

Noah was a *righteous* man. That means he had a *right* relationship with God. Noah obeyed God and did what God said was right. How about you? Do you obey God? Do you do what God says is right? Share one way you obey God.

_____

Noah walked with God. That means God was part of his everyday life. Noah listened and talked to God. He wanted to be pleasing to God. Do you make God part of your everyday life? Do you talk and listen to Him?

_____ Yes   _____ No

There is a very big difference in what we saw about man in Genesis 6 and Noah. Man's heart was evil, but Noah found favor in God's eyes. Do people see a difference in the things you do? Or do you talk, dress, go to movies, read books, and look at things on the Internet just like the people in the world who don't love God? Write out how you are different, how you find favor in God's eyes.

_____

_____

Write out how you are like the people in the world you live in.

_____

_____

Is there something you need to change? What shouldn't you be doing?

_____

WHO are you most like, *man* or *Noah?*

_____

That was a great discovery!

Tomorrow we'll find out how this big difference between Noah and man brought about God's first covenant. Don't forget to practice your memory verse. Say it out loud three times in a row, three times today.

GOD'S RESCUE

"Wow! So that's Masada! I can't believe we're going to hike up that huge rock at four o'clock in the morning!" Molly said as they hopped out of the Jeep at the bottom of Masada. "We are in the middle of nowhere!"

Uncle Jake laughed. "Masada is a natural rock fortress at the edge of the Judean Desert just west of the Dead Sea. It is 1,323 feet above the valley floor. Did you know that David lived in different strongholds (fortresses) in the wilderness when King Saul was trying to kill him? Some Bible scholars think Masada might be the stronghold mentioned in 1 Samuel 22:4.

"Every year schoolchildren in Israel make the climb at Masada just like we are going to do on our adventure today. Let's head over to 'snake path.' That's what the trail to the top is called."

Forty-five minutes later Max, Molly, Sam, and Uncle Jake reached the top of Masada a little hot and out of breath.

"Wow, we did it! We made it to the top!" Molly exclaimed.

Max pointed to the east. "Look! I see the Dead Sea. That's amazing." Then he turned around to look at the ruins of the city on the mountaintop. "I can't believe Herod the Great built a palace here as his refuge. Wasn't Herod the Great ruling here when Jesus was born?"

"Yes, he was," Uncle Jake replied.

"Isn't this also the city where Jewish rebels (the Zealots) took refuge when the Romans were conquering Israel from AD 72 to 74?"

"That's right, Molly." Uncle Jake pointed to a shady place. "Why don't we sit over there while we do some more exploring on God's first covenant?"

"That's a great idea," Max responded.

Since we marked the people in Genesis 6, we need to dig up the facts by asking the 5 W's and an H. Every treasure hunter knows how important the 5 W's and an H are to uncovering God's treasure. What are the 5 W's and an H, treasure hunter? They are the WHO, WHAT, WHERE, WHEN, WHY, and HOW questions.

1. Asking WHO helps you find out:

WHO wrote this?

WHO was it written to?

WHO are we reading about?

WHO said this or did that?

2. Asking WHAT helps you understand:

WHAT is the author talking about?

WHAT are the main things that happen?

WHAT is God telling you?

3. Asking WHERE helps you learn:

   WHERE did something happen?

   WHERE did the people go?

   WHERE was something said?

   When we discover a "WHERE," we double-underline the "WHERE" in green like we just did.

4. Asking WHEN tells you about time. Mark it with a green clock or a green circle like this ○. WHEN tells you:

   WHEN did this event happen or WHEN is it going to happen?

   WHEN did the main characters do something?

   WHEN helps us to follow the order of events.

5. Asking WHY asks questions like:

   WHY did the person say that?

   WHY did this happen?

   WHY did the person go there?

6. Asking HOW lets you figure out things like:

   HOW did something happen?

   HOW did the people react to what happened?

   HOW is something going to happen in the future?

   HOW does it come to pass?

Now that you know what the 5 W's and an H are, talk to your Expert Guide and ask for His help to discover His treasure.

Turn to page 199. Read Genesis 6:5-22. To uncover the treasure, ask the 5 W's and an H questions.

Genesis 6:5 WHAT was great on the earth?

_____

Genesis 6:6 HOW did the LORD feel about man?

_____

Genesis 6:7 WHAT is the LORD going to do?

_____

Genesis 6:11 WHAT was the earth like?

_____

Genesis 6:17 WHAT is God going to bring upon the earth?

_____

Genesis 6:17 WHAT is going to happen to all flesh that is on the earth?

_____

Genesis 6:18 WHAT is God going to establish?

_____

Genesis 6:18 WHO is the covenant for?

_____

Genesis 6:14,19 WHAT does God tell Noah to do?

Genesis 6:14 Make an _____ of _____

_____

Genesis 6:19 "Of every _____ thing of all flesh, you shall bring _____ of every _____ into the _____."

Genesis 6:19 WHY is it important for Noah to obey God? WHAT will the ark do for Noah, his family, and the animals?

_____

Isn't that *awesome?* Obeying God will save Noah and his family's lives. God has to judge man's sin, but because Noah has a right relationship with God, God will save him, his family, and some of the animals from being destroyed in the flood. This shows us that God is a loving and merciful God! He rescues those who love and follow Him.

Genesis 6:22 WHAT do we see about Noah? Did Noah obey?

_____

Incredible! Noah trusted and obeyed God even though it had never rained before (Genesis 2:5-6).

- Do you have faith in God like Noah did?

    _____ Yes   _____ No

- Are you willing to do what God asks you to do?

    _____ Yes   _____ No

- Do you trust God when something bad happens (like a flood)?

    _____ Yes   _____ No

- Do you believe that God loves you and will take care of you?

    _____ Yes   _____ No

- Write out one way that God shows He loves you.

_____

Way to go! You have cracked the first covenant code. You discovered that God made a promise to Noah. When God sends the flood to destroy the whole earth, He saves Noah, Noah's family, and some of the animals.

Now turn to page 37 and fill in the blanks on the chart for the first covenant we've discovered. Write out WHO made a covenant with WHOM. Then draw a picture to represent this covenant. For example, you might draw a picture of the ark to show that God promised to save Noah, his family, and some of the animals from the flood. Then fill in the blanks underneath the picture to tell what was promised.

All right! Don't forget to practice your memory verse. Say it out loud three times in a row, three times today, to remind you that God never forgets His promises.

A SiGN OF THE pROMiSE

Wasn't that an awesome hike up to Masada? Let's hop in the Jeep and pull out our treasure map of Israel to find the next location on our treasure hunt. Turn to page 11. The clue to our next location is "C-4." Look at the map. Find the letter C at the bottom, and put your right pointer finger on it. Then go up the left side of the map until you find the number 4. Put your left pointer finger on it. Move your right hand straight up and your left hand straight over until you find where the two intersect or meet. You have found the location!

WHAT is the next location for our treasure hunt?

_____

Way to go! Let's head out!

"Hmmm...Uncle Jake, is the Dead Sea also a clue in discovering more about covenant?" Max asked.

Uncle Jake grinned. "You're right, Max. The Dead Sea is not only our next location, but it is also the key word in our Key Word Secret Code that we will use to find out WHAT happened *after* the flood. WHAT happened when Noah and his family left the ark? Did God have anything else to say about covenant? Let's find out by cracking the code and looking at God's Map."

"You got it, Uncle Jake!" Molly replied as Sam barked and wagged his tail.

"Okay, guys," Uncle Jake instructed, "the first thing you need to do to crack the code is write out the key word like this:

D E A D   S E A

"Now cross off all the repeated letters. Max, what are we left with?"

"D-E-A-S," Max replied as he looked at his notebook.

"Good!" Uncle Jake continued. "Start the secret alphabet off with the letters that are left: D-E-A-S. After the letter S, write the regular alphabet but skip the letters that were left from the key word. After you finish, write the regular alphabet under the 'encoded' one, lining up the letters."

"I got it, Uncle Jake!" Max answered. "Here's our secret code."

Key Word Secret Code

D E A S B C F G H I J K L M N O P Q R T U V W X Y Z

A B C D E F G H I J K L M N O P Q R S T U V W X Y Z

Okay, treasure hunter, crack the code using the Key Word Secret Code to find out WHERE in God's Map you will find WHAT happened after the flood.

FBMBRHR MHMB: BHFGT-MHMBTBBM

_____ _____: _____ - _____

You did it! Don't forget to talk to God and ask for His help. Then grab those colored pencils so we can mark some key words in our Scripture passages.

What are *key words?* Key words are words that pop up more than once. They are called key words because they help unlock the meaning of the chapter or book you are studying and give you clues about what is most important in a passage of Scripture.

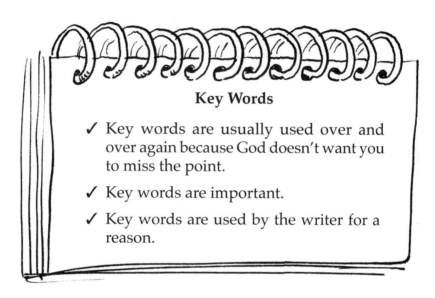

Key Words

✓ Key words are usually used over and over again because God doesn't want you to miss the point.

✓ Key words are important.

✓ Key words are used by the writer for a reason.

Once you discover a key word, you need to mark it in a special way using a special color or symbol so that you can immediately spot it in the Scripture, just like you did when you marked the people in Genesis 6.

Turn to page 200. Read Genesis 9:8-19 and mark these key words on your Observation Worksheets:

God (LORD) (draw a purple triangle and color it yellow)

Noah (and his sons) (color it blue)

covenant (draw a yellow box around it and color it red)

sign (draw a red stop sign around it)

flood (draw a wavy blue line over it)

Don't forget to mark your pronouns. And mark anything that tells you WHEN by drawing a green clock 🕐 or a green circle like this ◯.

Great! Now, ask those 5 W's and an H questions.

Genesis 9:8-9 WHO establishes the covenant?

_____

Genesis 9:9 WHO does God establish this covenant with?

_____

Genesis 9:11 WHAT is God promising in this covenant?

_____

Genesis 9:13 WHAT is the sign of the covenant?

_____

Genesis 9:14 WHEN will the bow be seen?

_____

Genesis 9:15 WHAT will God do when He sees the bow?

_____

Genesis 9:16 HOW long is this covenant for?

_____

Do you see why God gave this awesome sign of the covenant? Think about it. Before the flood, it had *never* rained. Now imagine what happens the next time a cloud comes up and it starts raining—but there is no ark to get into. Can you imagine how scary that would be? So, God establishes another covenant. God promises to never destroy the earth again with a flood. Then to remind Himself and all flesh of His promise, He gives them a sign. God puts a bow—a rainbow—in the cloud.

Have you ever seen a rainbow? Incredible, isn't it? The world looks at rainbows and thinks how pretty they are, but we know *the rainbow is a sign of God's promise* to never flood the earth again. The next time you see a rainbow, tell a friend that this is a sign of God's covenant— and God keeps His promises. He will never again destroy the earth with a worldwide flood.

Remember, God promised to save Noah, his family, and some of the animals (Genesis 6). And God did! He is faithful! He *always* keeps His promises!

How about you? Do you keep the promises you make? _____

Should you? _____

The next time you start to make a promise, remember *covenant* and how important promises are to God.

What a great find! Now turn to page 37. Fill in the chart for the covenant found in Genesis 9. Don't forget to draw a picture of the sign of the covenant, and then fill in the blanks about God's promise.

Practice your memory verse to remind you that God remembers His everlasting promise.

A SMOKING OVEN AND A FLAMING TORCH

"This is awesome, Uncle Jake!" Max exclaimed as he floated in the Dead Sea. "I can't believe we are floating *on* the water instead of sinking. Look at Sam bobbing up and down!"

"Did you know that the Dead Sea is the lowest place on earth? And did you also know it isn't called the 'Dead Sea' in the Bible?" asked Uncle Jake.

"What does the Bible call it?" Molly asked.

"The Bible calls it the 'Salt Sea,' the 'eastern sea,' and the 'sea of Arabah.' The reason people today call it the Dead Sea is that very few creatures can live in it because it is so full of mineral salts. That's why you float instead of sink."

"Look at this." Molly showed Max and Uncle Jake a handful of salt crystals from the water. "They look just like little snowballs."

"They sure do," Uncle Jake replied. "Okay, let's go shower and change clothes. The note said the next clue for our treasure hunt would be found at the Dead Sea. Are you ready to start looking?"

"We sure are!" Max and Molly replied.

"Race you to the showers!" Max yelled out as Sam ran beside him, playfully nipping at his heels.

Ten minutes later Molly ran out on the patio to find Uncle Jake and Max and Sam. "Look, guys! The next clue was in my locker. I wonder how it got in there?" She winked at Uncle Jake.

"Don't look at me." Uncle Jake gave Molly an innocent look. "What does the note say?"

"It's another code," Molly answered.

"I know how to crack this code." Max grinned. "All we need to do is color the spaces that have dots in them."

Here's the message, treasure hunter. Color the spaces that have a dot in them red. When you're done, you'll have the location in God's map for the next clue on covenant. Write the name of the place on the line below the code.

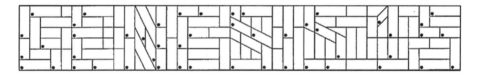

_____

Great decoding! Don't forget to talk to God.

Turn to page 201. Read Genesis 15 and mark the following key words on your Observation Worksheets:

God (LORD) (draw a purple triangle and color it yellow)

Abram (color it blue)

covenant (draw a yellow box around it and color it red)

land (double-underline it in green and color it blue)

believed (put a blue cloud around it)

Don't forget to mark your pronouns! And mark anything that tells you WHERE by double-underlining the WHERE in green. Mark anything that tells you WHEN by drawing a green clock or green circle like this ○.

Now, let's get the facts. Ask the 5 W's and an H questions.

Genesis 15:18 WHO made a covenant with WHOM?

The _____ made a covenant with _____

Genesis 15:18 WHAT was the promise made in this covenant?

To your _____ I have given this _____

Genesis 15:9 HOW was this covenant made? WHAT was done by WHOM?

G__ __ said to __ __ __ __ __, "Bring Me a _____

year old _____, and a _____ year old

_____ _____, and a _____ year old

_____, and a _____, and a _____

_____."

Genesis 15:10 WHAT did Abram do when he brought these to God?

Abram "c__ __ them in t__ __, and _____ each

half _____ the other; but he did not c__ __ the _____."

WHAT was shed when the animals were cut?

B__ __ __d!

Genesis 15:12 WHAT happened after the animals were cut and the sun was going down?

_____

_____

Genesis 15:17 WHAT happened after the sun had set?

"There appeared a _____ _____ and a _____ _____ which _____ between

these _____."

Wow! That's pretty cool! WHO is this smoking oven and flaming torch that passes between or through the pieces? We know it's not Abram because he is in a deep sleep. WHO do you think is appearing as a smoking oven and flaming torch?_____

Genesis 15:18 WHO is making the covenant?_____

Genesis 15:18 WHO is the covenant with?_____

Genesis 15:18 WHAT was God's promise (covenant) to Abram?

"To your _____ I have given this _____."

Genesis 15:18 says, "On that day the LORD made a covenant with Abram." Did you know that the word *made* in this verse is the Hebrew word *karath,* which means "to cut"? Remember how the animals were cut in two? *Cutting* implies the shedding of blood. God is the one who "cuts covenant" with Abram by passing between those pieces of flesh as a smoking oven and a flaming torch. God is making a solemn, binding agreement with Abram that cannot be broken. He is promising to give Abram descendants and the land. Later, when we study the New Covenant, we'll see WHOSE blood was shed and WHO passes through the pieces. That will be so awesome! So keep on studying!

Now turn to page 37. Fill in the chart for the covenant found in Genesis 15. Draw a picture showing God "cutting this covenant" with Abram. You might show Abram on the ground asleep while God, as a smoking oven and a flaming torch, passes through these bloody pieces of flesh.

Great work! You have discovered the treasure of three of God's covenants this week. Don't forget to say your memory verse out loud to a grown-up!

CHART ON COVENANTS	
Genesis 6:18 _____ establishes covenant with _____	Genesis 9:11 _____ establishes covenant with _____ and all _____
_____ promises to s__ __e Noah from the _____	There will never be another _____ to _____ the _____
Genesis 15:18 _____ made a covenant with _____	Genesis 17:7 _____ establishes His covenant between _____ and his _____
God's promise to Abram: To your _____ I will give this _____	Abram will be the father of a multitude of _____. God will give them the _____

CHART ON COVENANTS

Genesis 21:27 _____ made a covenant with _____	Genesis 26:26-28 _____ made a covenant with _____
Genesis 21:23 Swear by God you will not _____ _____ with me	Genesis 26:29 That you will do us _____ _____
Genesis 31:43-44 _____ made a covenant with _____	Exodus 34:27 _____ made a covenant with _____ and _____
Genesis 31:52 This heap and this pillar are a _____ that I will do you no _____ and you will do me no _____	Exodus 24:7 All that the _____ has spoken _____ _____ _____

CHART ON COVENANTS

Matthew 26:26-28 _____ makes a covenant for the world

This is My _____ of the covenant, which is poured out for many for the _____ of _____ .

TWO KINDS OF COVENANT

Hey, treasure hunter, it's great to have you back! Are you ready to continue hunting God's treasure?

Last week we discovered WHAT covenant is. We also uncovered three covenants God made with man. So far, God's covenants have been one way (God to man) and unconditional. Man hasn't done anything! God made each one of these covenants for man's benefit. God saved Noah and his family. And God promised to never flood the earth again. He gave a rainbow as a sign of His promise. God promised Abram descendants and land. Isn't that incredible?

WHAT will we discover this week? Let's continue our adventure to find out.

A SIGN OF THE COVENANT

"All right! We are packed and ready to go." Uncle Jake climbed into the Jeep. "Has anyone found the next clue for our adventure?"

"I did, Uncle Jake," Molly replied. "I found this clue wrapped in my napkin when we ate breakfast this morning."

"Ah ha!" Uncle Jake smiled. "Why don't you pull out the Israel treasure map and tell me where we're heading next."

Turn to the map on page 11. The clue to our next location is "C-5." Find the next location for our treasure hunt and write it down.

_____

Great work! Let's get on our way. But don't forget—first things first. Ask God for His help.

Uncle Jake looked into the rearview mirror at Max. "Okay, Mr. Cool. I know that if Molly got the map clue, you must have gotten the clue to the next location in our study on covenant."

"Who me?" Max burst out laughing. "I did get it, Uncle Jake." Max held out the clue. "What kind of code is this?"

"It's an alphabet code," Uncle Jake explained. "All you do to decode the message is write the letter that comes *before* the letter that is written in the regular alphabet."

Alphabet Code

A B C D E F G H I J K L M N O P Q R S T U V W X Y Z

Decode the message by looking at each letter in the secret message and writing the letter that comes *before* that letter in the alphabet on the line below the letter. For example, the first letter in our message is "H," so what letter comes before "H" in the alphabet? That's right. It's the letter "G." Crack the rest of the code so we know the next place we're going to find God's treasure.

Here's the secret message, treasure hunter. Can you solve it?

H F O F T J T   T F W F O U F F O

G_____   _____

You did it! Turn to page 202. Read Genesis 17:1-24 and mark these key words on your Observation Worksheets:

Abram (color it blue)

covenant (draw a yellow box around it and color it red)

sign (draw a red stop sign around it)

circumcised (draw an X)

Don't forget to mark the pronouns! And mark anything that tells you WHERE by double-underlining the WHERE in green. Mark anything that tells you WHEN by drawing a green clock or green circle like this: ◯ .

Now hunt for the treasure by asking the 5 W's and an H questions.

Genesis 17:1-2 WHO establishes the covenant with WHOM?

_____ establishes His covenant with

_____.

Genesis 17:4 WHAT is God going to make Abram the father of?

A multitude of _____

Genesis 17:7 WHO is this covenant between?

The covenant is between _____ and _____ and his _____.

Genesis 17:7 HOW long will this covenant last?

It is an _____ covenant.

Genesis 17:8 WHAT is to be given to Abraham and his descendants for an everlasting possession?

All the _____ of C__ __ __ __n

Genesis 17:9 WHAT are Abraham and his descendants to do?

They will _____ God's _____.

Genesis 17:10 HOW are they to keep the covenant? WHAT are they to do?

"Every _____ will be _____." (If you don't know what circumcision is, ask your parents.)

Genesis 17:11 WHAT is circumcision a sign of?

It's a sign of the _____.

Genesis 17:9 and 11 WHO is to be circumcised?

A__ __ __ __ __ __

Genesis 17:12-13 WHO else is to be circumcised?

"Every _____ among you who is _____ days old shall be circumcised throughout your _____" and "a _____ who is born in the house or who is bought with money from any foreigner."

Genesis 17:14 WHAT happens to the male who is not circumcised?

"That person shall be _____ _____ from his people."

Genesis 17:14 WHY will that happen?

He has _____ God's covenant.

Genesis 17:5 and 15 WHAT did God change?

Abram and Sarai's n__ __ __s

Genesis 17:16 HOW is God going to bless Abraham and Sarah?

"I will give you a _____ by her."

Genesis 17:16 HOW is God going to bless Sarah?

"She shall be a _____ of _____."

Genesis 17:19 WHO is God's covenant going to be through?

I__ __ __ __ and his d__ __ __ __ __ __ __ __ __ __

Genesis 17:23 WHEN was Abraham circumcised?

"In the very same _____"

Genesis 17:24 HOW old was Abraham when he was circumcised?

Did you notice how serious obeying God is? Circumcision showed the children of Abraham (who would later be called Jews) they were God's people. Circumcision was a sign, a reminder that they were a special people who were in covenant with almighty God. They *belonged* to God. If they refused to obey God and be circumcised, they were choosing to disobey Him and could not be His people.

Let's talk about our lives. Although circumcision was for the Jewish people, do you see how important it is to know God's Word and obey Him—even when it may be hard?

_____ Yes   _____ No

Way to go! We are sooooo proud of you for studying God's Word so you will know truth!

Turn to page 37, and fill in the chart for the covenant found in Genesis 17. Why don't you draw a picture of God's promise to Abram, that he would have a multitude of descendants and the land, to remind you of this covenant? Fantastic!

EXPLORING FOR TRUTH

"Look at all the caves!" Max exclaimed as they walked around Qumran.

"Oh no, Max!" Molly looked worried. "Remember what happened the last time you explored a cave in Israel? Let's not do that again."

"Don't worry, Molly," Uncle Jake said. "This time it's okay. I've arranged it so all of us can go inside one of the caves to experience what it might have been like when the young Bedouin boy discovered the clay jars that had the ancient scrolls hidden inside. And who knows? Maybe we'll find our next clue."

"This is incredible!" Max led Sam around the inside of a cave. Then Max looked at Molly. "Do you see any clues yet?"

"No," Molly replied. "Not yet. I'll go this way, and you and Sam check over there."

"I found it, Uncle Jake! Come over here, Molly. I found a big clay jar, and it looks like something is written on it."

WHAT is written on the jar, treasure hunter? Take a look. It's the same word we saw yesterday. Do you recognize it? If not, break the code by looking at the clue on the jar and decoding it by choosing the letter in the alphabet that comes before the letter in the clue just like you did yesterday.

HFOFTJT

"Uncle Jake, this clue tells us what book of the Bible we'll find the next treasure in, but it doesn't tell us which chapter or verse." Max said.

"Maybe there's another clue somewhere on the jar," Uncle Jake suggested.

As Max gently turned the jar, Molly knelt down to get a closer look. "I don't see anything, Max."

Max tilted the jar just a bit.

"Wait!" Molly exclaimed. "There's writing on the bottom! I'll get out my pen and notebook and write it down."

The three sets of numbers Molly wrote down reveal the next clue for finding God's treasure.

Look at the three sets of numbers on the bottom of the jar and write them on the lines next to the book of the Bible to reveal the three places we'll go to for our next treasure.

Genesis _____

Genesis _____

Genesis _____

(on jar: HFOFTJT)
(21:22-34)
(26:26-33)
(31:43-55)

Look at the first set of numbers on the jar. Pull out God's Map (the Bible). Read the passage, and then ask the 5 W's and an H.

Genesis 21:27 WHO makes a covenant with WHOM?

_____

Genesis 21:30 WHAT were the seven ewe lambs for?

_____

Genesis 21:31 WHAT did the two of them do when they made this covenant?

_____

Genesis 21:33 WHAT did Abraham plant?

_____

This is the first time we see man making a covenant with man. WHY did they make this covenant? Abimelech wants Abraham to show kindness to him, and Abraham wants the well he had dug that Abimelech's servants had taken over.

Turn to page 38, and fill in the blanks on the chart for this covenant in Genesis 21. Now draw a picture of the covenant. Fill in the blanks at the bottom to reveal the agreement between these two men.

Use God's Map to look up the second set of numbers on the jar. Look up and read the passage and answer these questions.

Genesis 26:26-28 WHO is the covenant between?

_____, with his adviser _____ and

_____ the commander of his army, and

I__ __ __ __

Genesis 26:30 WHAT did they do?

_____

Genesis 26:31 WHAT did they do the next morning?

They arose early and _____ _____.

First, Abimelech makes a covenant with Abraham. After Abraham dies, Abimelech wants to make a covenant with Abraham's son Isaac. Did you notice that in both of these covenants they made oaths to each other? And did you notice that both of these covenants were made because of fear and lack of trust?

Abimelech knows that Abraham and Isaac are blessed by the Lord, so he wants to make sure he's protected. He knows that a covenant is a solemn and binding agreement.

Turn to page 38, and fill in the blanks on the chart for this covenant in Genesis 26. Draw a picture of what these men did while establishing this covenant. Fill in the blanks at the bottom to reveal the agreement between them.

Now, let's look at the last set of numbers on the jar. Look up and read the passage in God's Map and answer the questions.

Genesis 31:43-44 WHO is making a covenant with WHOM?

_____ and _____

Genesis 31:49 WHAT does *Mizpah* mean?

"May the _____ between _____

and _____ when we are _____ one from the

other."

Genesis 31:50 WHAT is God?

_____

Genesis 31:52 WHAT was the heap a witness of?

Laban said, "I will not pass by this _____ to you

for _____, and you will not pass by this _____

and this _____ to me, for _____.

Genesis 31:53-54 WHAT did Laban and Jacob do on the mountain?

_____

_____

_____

Turn to page 38, and fill in the chart for the covenant in Genesis 31. Draw a picture of what these men did in this covenant. Then fill in the blanks at the bottom to show the agreement between these men.

Did you notice that God was a witness of this covenant? Jacob and Laban asked God to watch between them. This shows us how serious covenant is. We'll learn even more about the seriousness of covenant as we uncover more treasure.

So far we have seen two kinds of covenants. Covenants that God makes with man, and covenants that man makes with man.

Did you notice that God makes His covenants with man out of love, while man makes his covenants with man out of fear and distrust?

Let's help Max and Molly uncover this week's memory verse by looking at some broken pottery they found in the cave. Uncle Jake has labeled each broken piece or shard with a word. Can you figure out how the pieces should be glued back together to make a whole vase again? Match a pottery shard to the drawing, and then write the word from that piece where it goes on the vase. Then place the words in the order you'd read them on the jar on the blanks to discover your memory verse.

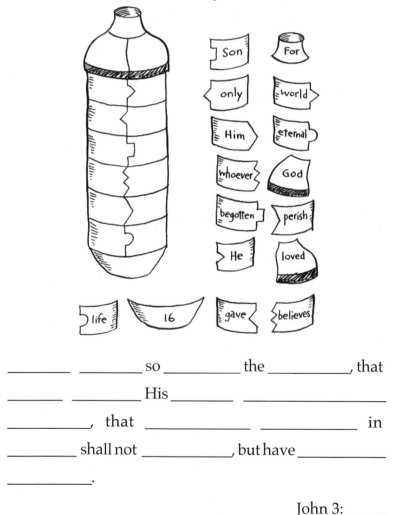

_____ _____ so _____ the _____, that

_____ _____ His _____ _____

_____, that _____ _____ in

_____ shall not _____, but have _____

_____.

John 3:_____

What a find! Wait until you see how this memory verse fits with God's New Covenant! Write this verse on an index card and practice saying it out loud three times in a row, three times a day.

DAY THREE

THE HUNT CONTINUES

"Boker tov!" That means "good morning" in Hebrew. Are you ready to head out on our next adventure now that we've discovered what Genesis has to say about covenant? Hop in the Jeep and grab your Israel treasure map (page 11). The clue to our next location is "B-5." Look at the map and write down where we are going.

_____

Great! Now talk to your Expert Guide. Then turn to page 204. Read Exodus 6:1-9 and mark the following key words on your Observation Worksheets:

God (LORD) (draw a purple triangle and color it yellow)

sons of Israel (Abraham, Isaac, and Jacob) (color it blue)

covenant (draw a yellow box around it and color it red)

land (this is the land of Canaan. Be careful to only mark the references that refer to the land of Canaan) (double-underline it in green and color it blue)

Don't forget to mark your pronouns! And mark anything that tells you WHEN by drawing a green clock ⏰ or green circle like this ◯ .

Let's hunt down the treasure!

Exodus 6:5 WHY are the sons of Israel groaning?

_____

Can you believe that the children of Israel—the descendants of Abraham, Isaac, and Jacob—are in bondage to the Egyptians? Remember what we discovered when we looked at the covenant God made with Abraham? God promised Abraham and his descendants the land of Canaan. But now Abraham's descendants are slaves in Egypt. Did God break His covenant?

Exodus 6:5 WHAT does God do?

God has _____ the _____ of the sons of

Israel. He r__ __ __ __ __ __ __ __d His _____.

Isn't that *awesome*? God heard the groaning of the sons of Israel and remembered His covenant. God is faithful!

Exodus 6:6 WHAT is God going to do since He heard their groaning and remembered His covenant?

_____

_____

Exodus 6:7 WHAT will God be to them?

_____

Exodus 6:8 WHAT will God give them?

_____

Exodus 6:9 HOW did the sons of Israel respond?

_____

Unbelievable! They didn't listen to God. They didn't believe God's promise. Isn't that sad? They were so discouraged that they quit trusting God. Has that ever happened to you? When something bad happened, did you wonder if God had forgotten about you? If that has happened, write down how you felt. For instance, did you feel alone or discouraged?

_____

_____

What did you do?_____

_____

_____

WHAT happens to the children of Israel? God delivers them! In Exodus 15, the children of Israel are out of bondage, Pharaoh and his army have drowned, and the Israelites are on their way to the land God promised them in His covenant. Remember this the next time you think God doesn't love you or has forgotten about you. God is faithful! He remembers His covenants!

Let's look at one more Scripture passage to find out what happens now that the sons of Israel are on their way to the promised land. Turn to page 205, and read Exodus 19:3-9. Moses has gone up a mountain to talk with God. Now read it again and mark these key words like you did before:

God (LORD)

sons of Israel

covenant

Also mark these key word phrases.

the words and all that the LORD has spoken (box these phrases in purple and color them green)

Now answer the following questions.

Exodus 19:5-6 WHAT are the words God speaks to the sons of Israel?

"If you will indeed _____ my v__ __ __ __ and _____ my _____, then you shall be My own _____."

Exodus 19:8 HOW did the people respond?

"_____ that the LORD has spoken we _____ _____!"

This time the people listened to Moses. They told God they would do what He said. Do you know WHAT the covenant is that God wants them to keep? You'll find out tomorrow as you continue to crack the covenant code.

Don't forget to practice your memory verse.

DISCOVERING THE OLD COVENANT

"Sam, get down! You're going to fall out of the Jeep hanging out like that." Max pulled Sam back inside and looked at Uncle Jake. "That was so cool getting to go inside the cave in Qumran. I'm sure it was a lot like what the Bedouin boy and the archeologists saw when they discovered the ancient scrolls."

"It was great," Molly agreed. "But I can't wait to see Jerusalem again. Where are we going first, Uncle Jake?"

Max ginned at Molly. "You know better than that. I'm sure Uncle Jake has hidden a clue somewhere in the Jeep for us."

Just then Sam jumped up to lick Max's face. Max noticed a piece of paper taped underneath Sam's collar. "Whoa! Wait a minute! What do we have here?" Max carefully removed the paper and unfolded it. "A clue! It looks like it is written in a number code or cipher."

"All right! Good job, Sam!" Molly exclaimed. "Let's decode it to find out where we're going next."

Okay, treasure hunter! Look at the secret message and decode it by finding the letter of the alphabet that matches the number in the Number Cipher Secret Code. Write down the letters on the blanks below the numbers.

Number Cipher Secret Code

A	B	C	D	E	F	G	H	I	J	K	L	M
2	4	6	8	10	12	14	16	18	20	22	24	26

N	O	P	Q	R	S	T	U	V	W	Y	X	Z
28	30	32	34	36	38	40	42	44	46	48	50	52

Secret Message

38—16—36—18—28—10   30—12   40—16—10   4—30—30—22

_____ _____ _____ _____

Did you figure out where we're going? We're heading to the Shrine of the Book. That's where they keep the Dead Sea Scrolls that were found in the caves in Qumran.

As we bounce around in the Jeep on the way to Jerusalem, let's look at the covenant God wants the children of Israel to keep. Don't forget to pray!

Turn to page 205. Read Exodus 24:3-12 and Exodus 34:27-28. Mark these key words in both passages.

God (LORD) (draw a purple triangle and color it yellow)

sons of Israel (Abraham, Isaac, and Jacob) (color it blue)

covenant (draw a yellow box around it and color it red)

all the words of the LORD (all the words which the LORD has spoken, all these words) (box them in purple and color them green)

Don't forget to mark your pronouns! And mark anything that tells you WHEN by drawing a green clock or green circle like this ◯ .

Look at Exodus 24 and 34. Ask the 5 W's and an H to solve the crossword puzzle on the next page.

Exodus 24:4 WHAT did Moses do?

1. (Down) He wrote down all the words of the _____.

2. (Across) He built an _____ at the foot of the mountain with twelve pillars for the twelve tribes of Israel.

Exodus 24:5 WHAT did the young men Moses sent do?

3. (Down) They offered burnt _____

4. (Down) and _____ young

5. (Down) _____ as

6. (Down) _____ offerings to the Lord.

Exodus 24:6 WHAT did Moses put in basins and sprinkle on the altar?

7. (Across) _____

Exodus 24:7 WHAT did Moses read in the hearing of the people?

8. (Across) The book of the _____

Exodus 24:7 HOW did the people respond?

9. (Down) "All that the LORD has spoken we will do, and we will be _____!"

Exodus 34:27 WHO is God making a covenant with?

10. (Across) God is making a covenant with _____ and with

11. (Across) _____.

Exodus 34:28 WHAT are the words of the covenant?

12. (Across) The _____ _____

Way to go!

WHAT do you see about this covenant that is different from the other covenants God made that we have looked at? This is a *two-way* covenant. It is *not* an unconditional covenant like the covenant God made with Abraham. This time *the people are expected to do something.*

Exodus 24:7 WHAT are the people expected to do? WHAT promise do they make?

"All that the _____ has _____ _____ _____

do, and we will be _____!"

You have just discovered the Covenant of Law—the *Old Covenant* that you probably know as the Ten Commandments.

Turn to page 38, and fill in the chart for Exodus 34:27, the Old Covenant. Draw a picture of Moses with the tablets of stone on Mt. Sinai.

Great discovery! Don't forget to practice your memory verse.

A NEW FIND—THE NEW COVENANT

"Wow, Uncle Jake! This is so amazing," Molly said as they walked around inside the Shrine of the Book and looked at the ancient scrolls.

"Look at this scroll on the book of Isaiah!" Max pointed to the case in front of him. "This is astounding. I can't believe we are looking at the oldest Bible manuscript ever found."

A lady from the museum approached Max and handed him a small clay jar—a replica of one of the clay jars the scrolls were found in. "Someone asked me to give this to a boy and girl with a wild pup. The person said to tell you that it will help you find a location in God's Map."

Max and Molly both laughed as Max took the jar. "That has to be us!" Max said. "We have the only wild pup allowed in this museum. Let's look inside, Molly. Wow! This time there are two messages."

"Let me see!" Molly said.

Max handed her two pieces of paper, and Sam jumped up, trying to grab them.

"The first one is written in the number cipher. The second one is a passage of Scripture. Let's go outside and decode the first message."

Number Cipher Secret Code

A	B	C	D	E	F	G	H	I	J	K	L	M
2	4	6	8	10	12	14	16	18	20	22	24	26

N	O	P	Q	R	S	T	U	V	W	Y	X	Z
28	30	32	34	36	38	40	42	44	46	48	50	52

Message #1
A Number Cipher

26—2—24—2—6—16—18   40—16—36—10—10   30—28—10

_____   _____   _____

Great decoding! Pull out God's Map (your Bible) to find out WHAT God has to say about covenant in Malachi 3:1.

Malachi 3:1 WHO is God going to send? WHO is coming?

The _____ of the _____

WHO is this? Read the second message from Max's clay jar—Matthew 26:26-29 (printed after the key words)—and mark these key words:

God (LORD) (draw a purple triangle and color it yellow)

Jesus (draw a purple cross and color it yellow)

covenant (draw a yellow box around it and color it red)

Message #2
Matthew 26:26-29

26 While they were eating, Jesus took some bread, and after a blessing, He broke it and gave it to the disciples, and said, "Take, eat; this is My body."

27 And when He had taken a cup and given thanks, He gave it to them, saying, "Drink from it, all of you;

28 for this is My blood of the covenant, which is poured out for many for forgiveness of sins.

29 But I say to you, I will not drink of this fruit of the vine from now on until that day when I drink it new with you in My Father's kingdom."

Matthew 26:26 WHAT did the bread represent?

_____

Matthew 26:27-28 WHAT did the cup represent?

_____

Matthew 26:28 WHY is Jesus' blood poured out? WHAT is the "blood of the covenant"?

_____

So WHO is the messenger of the covenant? WHO is God sending to make a covenant for us?

J__ __ __ __!

Isn't that *incredible*? Did you know that Jesus dying on the cross was a *New Covenant* God cut for us? What a terrific treasure! The God of the universe loves us so much that He sent His own Son to save us! *Jesus is the messenger of the New Covenant.* And the New Covenant says God will forgive us for all of our sins!

Turn to the Covenants Chart (page 39) and fill in the blanks for Matthew 26:26-28, the New Covenant. Draw a picture to show what God did for us!

You did it! Look at all the different covenants you discovered in just two weeks. You'll find out much more about these priceless treasures next week. Don't forget to say your memory verse out loud to a grown-up.

CUSTOMS OF COVENANT

Last week was incredible! Look at all we discovered about God's priceless treasure. We found out there are *two* kinds of covenant: covenants between God and man and covenants between man and man.

Were you surprised when you uncovered God's first "conditional covenant," the Old Covenant? This *Covenant of Law* required man to keep the Ten Commandments.

And you made quite a find when you discovered the New Covenant—a covenant of salvation. What a loving and merciful God to cut a covenant by sending His Son Jesus Christ to die for us!

So far in our quest for treasure, we have looked at the "big picture" of covenant. This week we will start uncovering the details. Let's find out about the customs of covenant.

CONTINUING THE QUEST

"*Boker tov*, Max," Uncle Jake said when Max walked into the kitchen.

"That sounds just like 'broken toe'!" Max laughed. "*Boker tov*, Uncle Jake. *Ma nishma*?" (Translation: "How are you?")

"*Metzuyan*, Max. That means 'excellent,' " Uncle Jake replied. "Your Hebrew is getting pretty good. Are you and Molly ready for our next adventure?"

"You better believe it!" Molly answered from where she was sitting at the table. "I found this clue when I poured my cereal this morning."

The clue Molly found was "C-6." Look at the Israel treasure map (page 11) and find it. Write down where we are going next.

All right! Grab Sam's leash and pile into the Jeep with Uncle Jake, Max, Molly, and Sam. Don't forget to ask God to lead us on this adventure.

As the Jeep headed down the road, Uncle Jake asked, "Do you remember the story of David and Goliath?"

"Sure," Max and Molly replied together.

"Did you know that after David killed Goliath, Abner, the commander of the Israeli army, took David to King Saul to hear about David's victory?" Uncle Jake asked.

"I didn't know that," Molly replied. "Did you, Max?"

"No, but..." Max smiled. "I've figured out the next clue! I bet whatever happens after David kills Goliath is going to help us uncover some of the customs of covenant."

"You got it, Max!" Uncle Jake gave Max the thumbs-up sign.

Okay, treasure hunter, turn to page 206. Read 1 Samuel 17:55-58 and 1 Samuel 18:1-5. Mark these key words in both passages:

David (color it blue)

Jonathan (color it orange)

love (draw a red heart)

covenant (draw a yellow box around it and color it red)

Don't forget to mark the pronouns. And mark anything that tells you WHEN by drawing a green clock ⏰ or green circle like this ◯.

WHAT did you learn about David? Look at every place you marked David on your Observation Worksheets. Make a list in your field notebook on what you discovered.

What I Learned About David

1 Samuel 17:55 David goes out against the

_____.

1 Samuel 17:55-56 David is a y__ __ __ __ man,

a youth.

1 Samuel 17:57 David k__ __ __ed the

P__ __ __ __ __ __ __ __ __ __.

1 Samuel 17:57 Abner took David before

_____. David has the Philistine's _____

in his hand.

1 Samuel 17:58 David is the son of Saul's servant

_____ the _____.

1 Samuel 18:2 Saul _____ David and did not

let him _____ to his _____ _____.

1 Samuel 18:5 David went out _____ Saul

_____ him, and _____.

1 Samuel 18:5 Saul set David over the _____

of w__ __.

Now, look at every place you marked *Jonathan* and list in your field notebook what you discovered about him.

What I Learned About Jonathan

1 Samuel 18:1 The s__ __ __ of Jonathan was knit to the s__ __ __ of __ __ __ __ __. Jonathan _____ David as himself.

1 Samuel 18:3 Jonathan made a _____ with _____.

1 Samuel 18:4 Jonathan gave David his _____, along with his _____, including his _____ and his _____ and his _____.

Good job, treasure hunter!

1 Samuel 18:3 WHY did Jonathan make this covenant with David?

_____

Isn't that awesome? Jonathan's motive for making this covenant was because he loved David! It wasn't because of fear or distrust like the other man-made covenants we've looked at.

Look at 1 Samuel 18:4. In the following box, draw the items Jonathan gave to David when he made the covenant with him.

Now number each item in the order Jonathan gave them to David on your Observation Worksheets (1 Samuel 18:4, on page 207).

WHY did Jonathan give David these things? Could giving David these things be a visual way to show what it means to be "in covenant" with someone? We'll find out as we uncover more of God's treasure.

Uh-oh! Watch out! Sam just jumped out of the Jeep. *Whew!* You got him! What did Sam find when he jumped out of the Jeep? Hey, it's a piece of paper with a number cipher! Break the code to discover your new memory verse.

Number Cipher Secret Code

A	B	C	D	E	F	G	H	I	J	K	L	M
2	4	6	8	10	12	14	16	18	20	22	24	26

N	O	P	Q	R	S	T	U	V	W	Y	X	Z
28	30	32	34	36	38	40	42	44	46	48	50	52

32—42—40   30—28   40—16—10   12—42—24—24

_____   _____   _____   _____

2—36—26—30—36   30—12   14—30—8   38—30

_____   _____   _____

40—16—2—40   50—30—42   46—18—24—24   4—10

_____   _____   _____   _____

2 4—24—10   40—30   38—40—2—28—8   12—18—36—26

_____   _____   _____

2—14—2—18—28—38—40   40—16—10

_____   _____

38—6—16—10—26—10—38   30—12   40—16—10

_____   _____   _____

8—10—44—18—24

_____ .

10—32—16—10—38—18—2—28—38

_____ 6:11

All right! Practice saying this verse out loud, three times in a row, three times today!

TWO BECOME ONE

"Wow, Uncle Jake!" Molly said as they climbed up the mountain at Bet She'an National Park. "This is really steep."

Sam ran ahead on the trail, turning around to bark at them as they hiked up the path.

"Okay, Sam, we hear you," Max scolded. "This is a steep mountain. We'll see you at the top. Uncle Jake, is this where the Philistine lords displayed the bodies of Saul and his sons on the city walls?"

"It sure is," Uncle Jake answered.

"That's so sad," Molly said. "Yesterday we saw Jonathan make a covenant with David, and today we are standing on the mountain in Bet She'an looking at the remains of the walls where the bodies of Jonathan, Saul, and Saul's other sons were hanged after they were killed by the Philistines."

"It is sad," Uncle Jake agreed. "Let's take a break and talk about what we've learned so far about covenant. We can sit over here."

"Well," Max said after sitting down, "we know covenant is a solemn and binding agreement between God and man or man and man. We saw how men who made covenants with each other promised to show kindness and not harm each another. And we know that once they made a covenant, they were responsible to protect each other."

"We also saw God save Noah from the flood. And He brought the children of Israel out of Egyptian bondage," Molly added. "It looks like there are both blessings and responsibilities that go with making a covenant."

"That's right." Uncle Jake nodded. "That's because covenant connects us to one another. It is two people becoming one. So when Jonathan gave David his robe, armor, sword, bow, and belt, maybe he was making a symbolic gesture to show they were connected to each other. David put on Jonathan's robe to identify himself with Jonathan. He was 'putting on Jonathan,' the son of the king."

"Hey, that's pretty cool," Max replied. "What about us? Last week we discovered God cut the New Covenant to save us. Is there something for us in the Bible that is similar to Jonathan and David exchanging robes and weapons?"

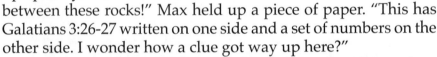

Uncle Jake winked at Max and Molly. "I guess you'll have to find out!"

"I wonder where we'll find the next clue?" Molly asked.

Max looked around and then got up quickly. "Look! I found it tucked between these rocks!" Max held up a piece of paper. "This has Galatians 3:26-27 written on one side and a set of numbers on the other side. I wonder how a clue got way up here?"

Max and Molly both looked at Uncle Jake. Sam jumped up and licked Uncle Jake's face.

Okay, treasure hunter, talk to God and then pull out God's Map. Look up Galatians 3:26-27. Hunt for the treasure by asking the 5 W's and an H questions.

Galatians 3:26 HOW are we sons of God?

Through _____ in _____ _____

Galatians 3:27 WHAT have we done if we have been "baptized into Christ" (believe in Jesus Christ as our Savior and have given our life to Him)?

_____ ourselves with _____

Doesn't that sound like David putting on Jonathan's robe? Jonathan cut a covenant with David, and then Jonathan gave

David his robe to put on to identify himself with Jonathan. God so loved the world that He sent His Son Jesus to save us from our sins. When we confess our sins and give our lives to Him, HOW are we clothed?

We are clothed with J__ __ __ __!

We get to wear Jesus' robe! We are changed. We have a new identity. We are in covenant with God through Jesus.

Are you ready to find the next clue? Break this secret code using the number cipher code you used in Day 1 of this week (page 69) so we will know where to find out more about who we are in Christ.

Secret Message

6—30—24—30—38—38—18—2—28—38   40—16—36—10—10

_____   _____

Now turn to page 207 and read Colossians 3:1-10. Mark these key words:

you (your, our) (color it orange)

put aside (lay aside) (circle it in red)

put on (circle it in blue)

Dig for treasure by asking the 5 W's and an H questions.

Colossians 3:3 WHAT has happened to your life now that you are a Christian?

"For you have _____ and your _____ is _____ with _____ in _____."

Colossians 3:8 WHAT are you to put aside?

"_____, _____, _____, _____, and

_____ _____ from your mouth."

Colossians 3:9 WHAT are you not to do?

"Do not _____ to one another, since you _____

aside the _____ _____ with its _____

practices."

Colossians 3:10 WHAT are you to put on?

The _____ _____

When God says "put on the new self" and lay "aside the old self," He is telling us when we are Christians we are to act like Jesus would act—not like we behaved before we believed in Jesus and became part of the New Covenant. For instance, do you know any kids who are bullies? Do these kids care about you? Do they love you and want what is best for you? No. They are being mean and cruel and they think it is fun and funny. Would Jesus do what they are doing? No way! So when they act like this, are they "putting on Jesus" or living for themselves?

_____

Have you ever acted like that? _____ Yes _____ No

If you have, which self did you have on?

_____

Look at the list of things we are to "put aside" again: anger, wrath (an outburst of anger like an explosion), malice (being mean and vicious), slander (insults, saying something untrue that puts someone down), and abusive speech (saying cruel things that tear people down and make them feel worthless).

When you are in covenant with Jesus, you are different because you have put on Jesus. Answer the following questions to see which self you are wearing.

Do I lose my temper?

_____Yes   _____ No   _____ Sometimes

Do I talk about other kids? Do I treat people ugly? Do I wish harm on anyone?

_____Yes   _____ No   _____ Sometimes

Do I say things that aren't true about other people?

_____Yes   _____ No   _____ Sometimes

Do I use bad language or talk mean to others? Do I text mean things about other people?

_____Yes   _____ No   _____ Sometimes

Do I lie or tell the truth?

_____

Am I greedy?

_____Yes   _____ No   _____ Sometimes

Do I keep myself pure or do I watch things on TV or the Internet that God says are wrong?

_____Yes   _____ No   _____ Sometimes

If you do some of the things God doesn't like, what are they?

_____

_____

Looking at your answers, have you laid aside your old self?

_____

Once we accept Jesus Christ as our Savior, we are to be different. We are not to do the bad things (sin) we used to. We are to be like Jesus. We are to put aside our old self and put on the new self. Like David put on Jonathan's robe, we are to put on Jesus.

WHAT are some ways you can put on the new self? Grab God's Map and look up and read Ephesians 4:22-32. List at least three ways you can put on Jesus.

1. _____

2. _____

3. _____

Is there anything God has shown you in your life that is part of the old self? Is there something you need to change? If you see something you need to change, all you have to do is tell God you are sorry for the things you are doing wrong and ask Him to forgive you. Then ask Him to help you put on Jesus.

Way to go! Don't forget to practice your memory verse. And the next time you change your clothes, get dressed in the morning, or get ready for bed at night, remember that if you have accepted Jesus Christ as your Savior, you have been saved. You are identified with Christ. You have put on Jesus! Live like He would!

Are you ready to find out where our adventure will take us tomorrow? Grab your Israel treasure map (page 11). Find "B-5" and write where we're going to find our next clue on covenant.

_____

And what are we going to visit when we arrive at that location? Crack the following number cipher to find out. (The code key is on page 69.)

40—16—10   14—2—36—8—10—28   40—30—26—4

_____   _____   _____

DAY THREE

A NEW FiND!

"This is amazing! I can see what looks like eyes and a nose in that craggy rock. It looks just like a skull," Molly said as they took

a closer look at the cliff near the Garden Tomb. "I never imagined Jesus was crucified so close to a road."

"Is this really where Jesus was crucified?" Max asked Uncle Jake.

"We really don't know for sure. Some people think it happened where the Church of the Holy Sepulchre is today— that's considered the traditional site. And some people think it happened here because it fits the land descriptions found in the Bible. We do know Golgotha was probably on a road like this because it was the custom of the Romans to punish people by main roads. We also know that it happened outside the city, and that an unused rock tomb was nearby, such as the Garden Tomb. But there isn't any proof that either of these locations is the actual place. But isn't the Garden Tomb a great place for us to think about what Jesus did for us?"

"Just think," Molly said as they walked inside to see the empty tomb, "Jesus could have been lying right there."

Uncle Jake smiled. "Doesn't it thrill your heart to know Jesus died for your sins but He didn't stay dead? Look at this sign: 'He is not here—For He is risen'!"

"Hey," Max said as they climbed out of the tomb, "a man handed me an envelope."

 "Open it, Max. Let's see what's inside," Molly said.

Max opened it. "There are two clues," he said. "Clue number one reads, "Being found in appearance as a man."

"Hmmm." Molly thought for a minute. "That's a Bible verse in Philippians. We need to find it so we can continue our treasure hunt."

"Good thinking, Molly," Uncle Jake added. "Yesterday we found out that when we accept Jesus Christ as our Savior, we are changed and become a new creation in Him. We put on a new self. We change robes with Jesus. But we didn't find out if Jesus changed robes and 'put on us.' This clue will help us find out if Jesus changed robes with us."

Okay, treasure hunter! Talk to God. Then read Philippians 2:5-8 (printed after the key word information). Mark this key word:

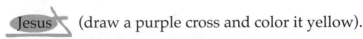 (draw a purple cross and color it yellow).

And don't forget to mark the pronouns! Let's find out if Jesus puts our robe on.

Philippians 2:5-8

5 Have this attitude in yourselves which was also in Christ Jesus,

6 who, although He existed in the form of God, did not regard equality with God a thing to be grasped,

7 but emptied Himself, taking the form of a bond-servant, and being made in the likeness of men.

8 Being found in appearance as a man, He humbled Himself by becoming obedient to the point of death, even death on a cross

List in your field notebook what you learn about Jesus.

What I Learned About Jesus

Philippians 2:6 [Jesus] existed in the _____ of _____. He "did not regard _____ with _____ a thing to be grasped."

Philippians 2:7 [Jesus] "_____ Himself, taking the _____ of a _____-_____, and being made in the _____ of _____."

Philippians 2:8 Jesus was "found in appearance as a _____, He _____ Himself by becoming _____ to the point of _____."

Philippians 2:6 WHO was Jesus?

Jesus existed in the _____ of _____.

Did you know that? Jesus is G ___ ___!

Philippians 2:7 WHAT did Jesus put on? HOW was Jesus made?

"In the _____ of _____"

Do you believe it? *Jesus is God!* And He put on our robe by becoming a human being. Jesus who was and is God became a man. Do you know WHY Jesus became a man to save us? Let's find out by looking at the next clue Max was given.

"It's time to see what clue number two is!" Uncle Jake said.

"'Therefore, He had to be made like His brethren in all things,'" Max read. "This is from the book of Hebrews."

Read Hebrews 2:14 and 17-18 (printed after the key word) and mark this key word:

Jesus (draw a purple cross and color it yellow)

Hebrews 2:14

14 Therefore, since the children share in flesh and blood, He Himself likewise also partook of the same, that through death He might render powerless him who had the power of death, that is, the devil.

Hebrews 2:17-18

17 Therefore, He had to be made like His brethren in all things, so that He might become a merciful and faithful high priest in things pertaining to God, to make propitiation for the sins of the people.

18 For since He Himself was tempted in that which He has suffered, He is able to come to the aid of those who are tempted.

Hebrews 2:14 WHY did Jesus become flesh and blood?

_____

_____

Hebrews 2:17 WHY did he have to be like us?

_____

_____

Hebrews 2:18 WHY is Jesus able to come to our aid?

_____

Jesus had to become like us so He could die in our place to pay for our sins and set us free from the power of the devil. Sin gives the devil his power, but Jesus paid for our sins so we can be set free from sin. Jesus exchanged robes with us. He put on our ugly, dirty robes of sin by dying on the cross and becoming sin for us. And we get to put on His beautiful robe of righteousness. Jesus put on our robe so we could put on His and be made right with God. *Isn't that incredible?*

Have you accepted this *awesome* gift of salvation from God? If you haven't and you want to, the first thing you need to do is know WHO Jesus is and believe it. You have to...

- believe Jesus is God's Son

- believe Jesus is God

- understand that when Jesus lived as a man, He lived a perfect life without sinning

- believe Jesus died on a cross to pay for our sins

- believe Jesus was buried, and God raised Him three days later from the dead

- believe you are a sinner and that you need someone to save you because you can't save yourself

- repent—to repent means to change your thinking, to change your mind about sin and your need for a Savior

- confess to God that you are a sinner, and tell Him you want to turn away from sin

- be willing to turn away from doing things your way, and start obeying Jesus. You have to turn your entire life over to God to become a follower of Jesus Christ and let Jesus have complete control over your life

Take some time to think about what you have learned about WHO Jesus is and WHAT He has done for you. If you truly believe in WHO Jesus is, WHAT He did for you, and know you are a sinner who cannot save yourself, ask: *Am I ready to give my life to Jesus and let Him take over my life?*

If you are ready, then go to a grown-up and ask them to help you take that step.

Now that you have discovered WHO Jesus is and HOW He put on your robe so you could wear His, write out a prayer to Him. Tell Jesus thank you for leaving heaven to become a man so that you could be saved and wear His robe of righteousness. Remember, Jesus was tempted but He did not sin. He will help you be like Him!

_____

_____

_____

_____

_____

Way to go! We are so proud of you! What an awesome day! Why don't you sit outside and think about all the wonderful things Jesus did for you? And don't forget to practice your memory verse!

WEAPONS EXCHANGE

Wasn't it exciting to go to Golgotha where Jesus might have been crucified and to walk into the empty Garden Tomb? Yesterday we hunted down clues to the treasure and found out that Jesus became a man so He could exchange robes with us.

Today we need to find out about the other things (besides his robe) Jonathan gave David. But before we get started, let's look at the other treasure map—the map of Jerusalem—to find our next location. Turn to page 94. Our next location in Jerusalem is "J-5." Locate it on the map and write down where our next adventure will be.

_____

Now hop into the Jeep and then talk to your Expert Guide.

We are on our way! Turn to page 207. Read 1 Samuel 18:4 to help you remember the other things Jonathan gave David.

1 Samuel 18:4 WHAT were the other things Jonathan gave David?

Jonathan gave David his robe, with his _____, including his _____, his _____, and his _____.

WHY did Jonathan give David his armor? Look at the armor. The armor included Jonathan's sword, bow, and belt—his weapons. Jonathan gives David his armor because they have a common enemy: the Philistines. Jonathan is giving David his armor to fight the enemy.

Is God's Word showing us a picture of something that affects us too? Do we have an enemy? Let's find out! Pull out God's Map. Look up and read 1 Peter 5:8.

1 Peter 5:8. WHO is our adversary?

_____

Jesus Christ and man have a common enemy. WHO is it? The devil! WHAT is our enemy like? Look up and read John 8:44, and then fill in what you learned in your field notebook.

What I Discovered About the Devil

He was a _____ from the beginning.

He does not stand in the _____.

There is no _____ in him.

He is a _____ and the father of _____.

Good job! Now look up and read 1 John 5:19. WHO does the whole world lie in the power of?

_____

Does the world love God? No! Does the world believe that Jesus is the only way to God? No! Look up and read James 4:4.

James 4:4 WHAT is the world?

An e__ __ __ __ of God

Did you know that? When Adam and Eve sinned in the Garden of Eden, Satan became the prince of this world. Then Jesus came to earth to defeat Satan and his power over man. Jesus defeated Satan when He paid for man's sins by dying on the cross and rising from the grave.

Until Jesus comes back again, we are in a war with Satan. HOW do we fight this war? Jonathan gave David his armor. Jesus helps us too. Let's find out about the armor Jesus gives us.

Turn to page 208. Read Ephesians 6:10-17 and mark these key words:

(put on) (take up) (circle it in blue)

(armor) (circle it in brown)

stand firm (box it in orange)

devil (the evil one, rulers, powers, and forces) (draw a red pitchfork)

Discover the treasure by asking the 5 W's and an H questions.

Ephesians 6:10 HOW are we to be strong?

_____

Ephesians 6:12 WHO is our struggle against?

"Against the _____, against the _____, against the

_____ _____ of this _____, against

the _____ _____ of _____

in the _____ _____."

Ephesians 6:11 WHAT are we to put on?

_____

Ephesians 6:11 WHOSE armor is it? _____

Ephesians 6:11 and 13 WHAT will the armor enable us to do?

_____

_____

Ephesians 6:14-17 WHAT is the armor we need to put on?

"Stand firm therefore, having _____ your loins

with _____, and having put on the _____

of _____, and having shod your

_____ with the preparation of the _____

of _____; in addition to all, taking up

the _____ of _____…And take the _____

of _____, and the _____ of the _____,

which is the _____ of _____."

Look at 1 Samuel 18:4 on page 207. WHAT was Jonathan's armor? His _____, his _____, and his _____.

HOW many of these pieces of armor do we have? _____

We didn't see a bow in our list, but look at Ephesians 6:16. WHAT is the devil shooting at us?

_____

Ephesians 6:16 HOW are we to put these arrows out?

With the _____ of _____

What about the belt? Did you know that the belt holds all the pieces of armor in place? It was a symbol of strength. Ephesians 6:14 says, "Having girded your loins with truth," which means "having put on the belt of truth."

What did we learn about our enemy in John 8:44? He is a liar because there is no truth in him. So when Satan comes after us, we need to fight him with the truth. HOW do we know what truth is? By knowing God's Word! You are putting on and tightening your "belt of truth" right now by studying God's Word!

Ephesians 6:17 WHAT did we learn about the sword?

_____

Are you using your sword? Do you know God's Word?

Do you know there is Someone who is called the "Word of God," Someone who will judge and wage war? WHO is this person?

Grab God's Map. Look up and read Revelation 19:11-16.

Revelation 19:11 and 13 WHO is called the "Word of God"?

_____

Revelation 19:11 WHO is coming on a white horse one day very soon?

_____

Revelation 19:16 WHO is the "King of kings, and Lord of Lords"?

_____

Isn't that *awesome*? It's *Jesus!* When we enter into covenant with God through Jesus Christ, we have a common enemy—

Satan. But we don't have to worry because *God has given us His armor* to fight the enemy with. We have the shield of faith to put out the devil's flaming arrows. We have the belt of truth—God's Word. It is our strength. And we have the sword of the Spirit, which is God's Word, to fight our enemy. And one day very soon, the "Word of God" will come again to banish our enemy forever. And then we will rule and reign with Jesus!

We can't wait! But until then, remember WHO you are in covenant with, tighten your belt of truth, and stand firm in the Lord in the strength of His might.

TRACKING THE ENEMY

"We're here!" Molly said as Sam barked and tried to jump out of the Jeep. "Oh no you don't! Get back inside, boy. We'll be in big trouble if you get loose on the Temple Mount. One of those soldiers might just shoot you!"

"Good work, Molly!" Uncle Jake said. "Okay, let's put on our credentials—our passes that show we are authorized to be here—so we can get through security and find our next clue."

After they donned their badges, they walked to the Temple Mount entrance and went through the security gate.

"Look!" Molly picked up her bag after it came through the security scanner. "Did you see that? Someone put something in my backpack's side pocket. I bet it's our next clue!" She dug it out.

"All right!" Max exclaimed as he looked over Molly's shoulder. "Let's crack the code."

Okay, treasure hunter, you know what to do. Color the spaces red that have a dot in them. Write what you uncover on the line below the puzzle.

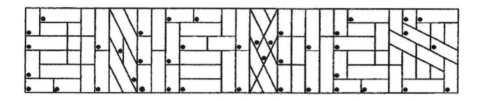

Great decoding! We need to find out more about covenant partners' enemies. Yesterday we found out that when we enter into a covenant with someone, that person's enemies become our enemies.

Today we need to find out WHO becomes WHOSE enemy as we take another look at the covenant between Jonathan and David. We'll also find out more about being in covenant with Jesus.

In God's Map, look up and read 1 Samuel 18:3-11 and 28-29.

> 1 Samuel 18:7-8 WHAT makes Saul angry? WHAT does Saul think David will get?

Saul's k__ __ __ __ __ __

Uh oh. It looks like Saul is jealous of David.

> 1 Samuel 18:29 WHO is David's enemy? _____

Look up and read 1 Samuel 19:1-2.

> 1 Samuel 19:1 WHAT does Saul want to do to David?

_____

> 1 Samuel 19:2 WHAT does Jonathan tell David to do?

_____

_____

In God's Map, look up and read 1 Samuel 20:12-16 and 23.

1 Samuel 20:13 WHAT will Jonathan do if he finds out his father wants to harm David?

S__ __ __ David a__ __y, that he may go in _____.

WHY would Jonathan help David when Saul was his father?

1 Samuel 20:16 WHAT had Jonathan made with David?

A _____

How cool is that? If Saul wants to kill David, Jonathan is going to send his friend away so he will be safe. Jonathan will protect his covenant partner from his father, King Saul.

How about God? Does God protect you when you are in covenant with Him?

Turn to page 208. Read John 15:17-19 and mark these key words:

Jesus (I, Me, My) (draw a purple cross and color it yellow)

you (color it orange)

world (draw a circle with two wavy lines inside)

love (draw a red heart)

hate (draw a black heart)

Now, uncover the treasure by asking the 5 W's and an H questions.

John 15:18 HOW does the world feel about Jesus?

_____

John 15:19 HOW does the world feel about us because we are Jesus' friends?

_____

When we are in covenant with God, WHO becomes our enemy?_____

Turn to page 208. Read John 17:14-17 and mark these key words:

Your word (color it purple)

world (draw a circle with two wavy lines inside)

hated (draw a black heart)

evil one (draw a red pitchfork)

This is Jesus' prayer for His disciples before He is arrested.

John 17:14 WHO hates "them"? The _____

John 17:15 WHAT does Jesus ask God to do?

"_____ them from the _____ _____"

That means that Jesus wants God to keep us out of the power of the evil one. How awesome! Jesus is asking God to take care of us in a world that is an enemy of God.

In God's Map, look up and read 1 John 2:15-17.

> 1 John 2:15 If the world is our enemy, are we to love
> the world?

_____

Loving the world means believing and doing things the world says are okay but God says are wrong. We "love the world" when we do things the Bible says we shouldn't do—when we do what people around us are doing that God says is wrong (sin).

Some of your friends and other kids will want you to look like them, act like them, talk like them, and do the things they think are okay. They don't want you to be different. But if you are in _covenant with Jesus_, you are not to be like the people living in the world. Instead, you are to be like Jesus.

Do you know if you love the world? How do you dress? How do you talk? What do you look at on the Internet or text on your phone? How do you treat your parents? Write out what you do.

_____

_____

_____

> 1 John 2:15 WHAT isn't in us if we love the world and
> the things of the world?

> The _____ of the _____

Is God's love in you? Do you have a relationship with Jesus? Have you given your life to Jesus? _____

If you have given your life to Jesus, can you be friends with Jesus and the world?

_____

Is the world your friend or enemy? _____

Are you going to stand on God's side (do what God says is right) or on the world's side (go along with and do what the world says is right)?

_____

If we love Jesus and have become partners with Him in the New Covenant, His enemies are our enemies. We are Jesus' friends. We are not to love this world. We are to do what God says is right. We are to live for Jesus!

You have done an awesome job this week. Now, don't forget to say your memory verse out loud to a grown-up. Ask them if they know how to put on their armor.

TREASURE MAP OF JERUSALEM

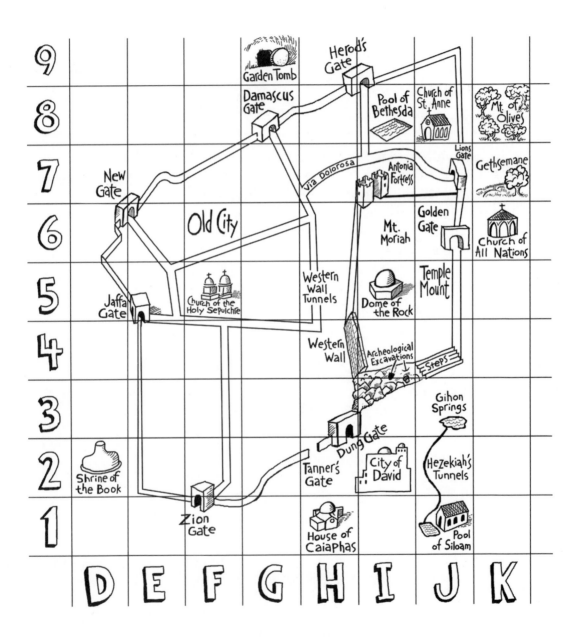

THE SERIOUSNESS OF COVENANT

Wow! Wasn't it great to find out when we enter into covenant with God through Jesus Christ that we get to put on His robe? We get to exchange our dirty robes of sin for His beautiful robe of righteousness. Isn't it amazing that Jesus loves us so much that He put on our robe by becoming a man just so He could save us?

And we learned that when we enter into covenant, our covenant partner's enemies become our enemies. We also learned how to put on the armor of God to help us stand firm and defeat the devil.

What will we uncover this week? Let's head to the Temple Mount in Jerusalem to find out.

A PLEDGE

"Did you know that the Temple Mount is on Mount Moriah, which is where Abraham offered his son Isaac to God?" Molly asked Max as they walked across the Temple Mount. "And did you know that it's also where David built an altar on the threshing floor of Araunah the Jebusite?"

"I sure did!" Max answered. "It's also where Solomon built the first temple that Nebuchadnezzar destroyed when he took the sons of Israel into captivity. After the captivity was over, Zerubbabel built the second temple, which Herod the Great rebuilt and expanded. The Romans destroyed that temple in AD 70." Max looked up. "Hey! Do you see that golden dome? That's the Dome of the Rock. It's built where the temple used to be and where the Bible says the new temple will be built in the future."

"Great work, you two!" Uncle Jake patted Max and Molly on their backs. "I'm so proud of you. You have done a great job studying the Bible. Isn't it fun seeing the places you've been learning about?"

"It's great, Uncle Jake." Molly smiled. "Thanks for the treasure hunt."

"We still have a lot more to discover. What does your guidebook say about the Temple Mount, Max?" Uncle Jake asked.

When Max turned to the page in his guidebook about the Temple Mount, a piece of paper fell out.

"What's that?" Molly asked. "What does it say?"

"It's another alphabet code," Max replied. "Let's crack the code."

Alphabet Code

A B C D E F G H I J K L M N O P Q R S T U V W X Y Z

Treasure hunter, do you remember how to do this code? You pick the letter of the alphabet that comes *before* the letter that is written below.

GJSTU   TBNVFM   UXFOUZ

_____   _____   _____

Fantastic! Now turn to page 209 and read that chapter. Mark these key words:

David (color it blue)

Jonathan (color it orange)

King Saul (father) (circle it in black)

covenant (agreement, has sworn) (draw a yellow box around it and color it red)

Don't forget to mark the pronouns. And mark anything that tells you WHERE by double underlining the WHERE in green. Mark anything that tells you WHEN by drawing a green clock or green circle like this ◯.

Uncover God's treasure by asking the 5 W's and an H questions.

1 Samuel 20:1 WHAT is David's concern?

_____

_____

1 Samuel 20:8 WHY does Jonathan need to deal kindly with David?

_____

Remember what we learned last week when Jonathan and David exchanged weapons?

"Your e__ __ __ __ __ __ are my e__ __ __ __ __ __."

1 Samuel 20:13 WHAT will happen if Jonathan doesn't protect David from his father's anger and desire to harm David?

_____

_____

Wow! Jonathan is pledging that the Lord will bring harm on him if he doesn't keep his covenant by protecting David.

1 Samuel 20:15-16 WHO did this covenant include?

The covenant was between Jonathan's h__ __ __ __ and

the h__ __ __ __ of David.

1 Samuel 20:23 Because of the covenant (agreement), WHO will be between Jonathan and David?

_____

1 Samuel 20:23 HOW long will this covenant last?

_____

1 Samuel 20:42 WHAT does Jonathan tell David to do?

"Go in _____."

1 Samuel 20:42 WHAT did they swear "in the name of the Lord"?

"The _____ will be _____ _____ and _____, and

between my _____ and your _____

_____."

Incredible! WHAT does this promise they swore to each other mean? We'll find out as we continue to hunt for God's treasure.

Guess what? Max and Molly discovered another message written on a drawing of the Western wall inside their guidebook. Crack the code by unscrambling the mixed-up words written on the stone wall and placing the words in order in the blanks below to uncover this week's memory verse.

PAHMIZ EH DSAI YMA
RDLO CHWAT ENBETWE
OUY EM ENTABS
EON THERO ISGENES

And _____, for _____ _____, " _____

the _____ _____ _____ _____

and _____ when we are _____ _____

from the _____."

_____ 31:49

You did it! Write this verse out on an index card and practice saying it out loud three times in a row, three times today.

A WITNESS

"Here we are at the Western Wall," Uncle Jake said. "Did you know that archeologists think this is the only part of the temple wall that Titus, the Roman general, didn't destroy in AD 70? There is no holier place for the Jews today than this wall because it was the closest to the holy of holies in the temple. The Jewish people gather here to cry, pray, sing, and chant portions of Scripture."

"That's amazing." Max looked around. "May we stand at the wall and pray, Uncle Jake?"

"We sure can. It's special to get to stand this close to God's most holy place, but first you need to put on this *yarmulke* to cover your head. Jewish men wear these when they eat, pray, or study. And because this is a holy site, all men have to have their heads covered. The wall area is divided so there is a side for the men and a side for the women. Molly, you'll have to go to the women's side to pray. Max, you and I will go to the men's side. Molly, keep next to us on the other side of the screen. And we'll meet back here in 20 minutes, okay? Let's go pray."

After 20 minutes, Uncle Jake, Max, and Sam met Molly at the corner of the square.

"That was so cool standing next to all those men of different nations, especially the Jewish men, to pray at the wall," Max said as he took off his yarmulke. "Hey, wait a minute! I didn't notice this when I put it on, but there's a message written in code inside my yarmulke."

Where was the code found? In Max's y__ __ __ __ __ __e. That's the clue for the next secret code. It's another Key Word Secret Code using the key word "yarmulke" to start off the alphabet. Max and Molly put "yarmulke" at the beginning of the alphabet and then left out the letters in that word when they wrote out the regular alphabet. Use their Key Word Secret Code to decode the secret message.

Key Word Secret Code

Y A R M U L K E B C D F G H I J N O P Q S T V W X Z
A B C D E F G H I J K L M N O P Q R S T U V W X Y Z

What does the secret message say, treasure hunter?

Key Word Secret Message
G B Z J Y E

All right! That is our clue. Today we're going to take another look at the covenant that Jacob made with Laban to find out what *mizpah* means.

Turn to page 212. Read Genesis 31:43-55 and mark the following key words:

covenant (draw a yellow box around it and color it red)

witness (circle it in blue)

The Lord watch between you and me (box it in purple)

Now ask the 5 W's and an H questions to solve the crossword.

Genesis 31:43-44 WHO is this covenant between?

1. (Down) _____ and

2. (Across) _____

Genesis 31:44 WHAT is the covenant?

3. (Across) A _____ between Jacob and Laban.

Genesis 31:45 WHAT did Jacob do with the stone?

4. (Across) He set it up as a _____.

Genesis 31:46 WHAT did they do with the stones that they gathered?

5. (Across) They made a _____.

Genesis 31:46 WHAT did they do by the heap?

6. (Down) They _____.

Genesis 31:48 WHAT is the heap?

7. (Down) A _____

Genesis 31:49 WHAT does *mizpah* mean?

8. (Across) "May the _____

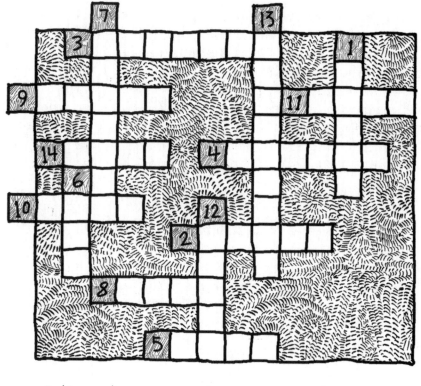

9. (Across) _____ between you and me."

Genesis 31:52 WHAT was the heap and the pillar a reminder of?

10. (Across) "I will not _____ by this heap to you for

11. (Across) _____, and you will not pass by this heap and this pillar to me, for harm."

Genesis 31:53 WHAT is God going to do?

12. (Down) _____ between them

Genesis 31:54 WHAT did Jacob offer?

13. (Down) A _____

Genesis 31:54 WHAT did they do together after that?

14. (Across) "They ate the _____ and spent the night on the mountain."

Great work! Did you notice how Jacob and Laban set up a pillar and a heap to be a witness? This witness was to remind them of their covenant to each other. It's just like God giving the sign of the bow in the cloud and the sign of circumcision to remind the people of His covenants.

Isn't it cool how God tells us what *mizpah* means right in the Scripture? "May the Lord watch between you and me." Think about what Jonathan said to David. (If you can't remember, look up 1 Samuel 20:16 and 23.) Does this sound like *mizpah*?

Mizpah is a very serious statement. It means "calling on" or asking the Lord to deal with you if you don't keep the covenant you made. God is the witness and the judge. He will be the one to judge you if you break the covenant. Breaking a covenant has very serious consequences. We'll discover more about this as we continue our quest for God's treasure. Don't forget to practice your memory verse.

DAY THREE

KEEPING THE COVENANT

"Sam! Come back here!" Max yelled as Sam ran through a small sidewalk café in the Old City. "Quick, Molly! Cut him off. Oh no! He snatched that man's falafel."

"Whew! Thanks, Molly." Max said. Then he turned to the man who was staring at Sam. "Silcha, sir. May I buy you another one?"

"*Toda raba,* Max. That means 'thank you very much.' "

Max was shocked the man knew his name.

"Your Uncle Jake asked us to meet you here," the man said as he pointed to the two other men at the table. "I wasn't quite ready for Sam though."

"Who is!" Uncle Jake said as he walked up. He shook hands with the three men.

"Ami, Eitan, and Avi, this is Max and Molly." Uncle Jake said, making the introductions. "And you just met Sam. Max and Molly, this is Ami. He is one of the best tour guides in Israel. And these are his friends, who are also great tour guides."

Ami looked at Max and Molly. "I believe Sam stole your next clue when he grabbed my falafel."

"What is falafel?" Molly asked.

"Falafel is a sandwich made out of ground chickpeas and vegetables. It is deep fried and stuffed in a pita or pocket bread," Ami replied.

"Max, why don't you and Molly look around to find the envelope with your next clue in it?" Uncle Jake said.

"Here it is!" Molly said a few minutes later. She held up an envelope she'd found by the door of the cafe.

Okay, treasure hunter. Where are we going to go next in our search for treasure on covenant? Open the envelope and find out by using the same Key Word Secret Code you used yesterday (page 101).

Key Word Secret Message

PURIHM   PYGSUF   HBHU

_____   _____   ____

"Before we get started, let's think about what we learned about Jonathan and David when we studied 1 Samuel 20," Uncle Jake said.

Molly spoke up. "Jonathan and David made another covenant that included both of their houses, meaning their descendants."

"Great, Molly. Jonathan knew that God had appointed David to be the next king of Israel. So he asks David to make a covenant with him to make sure that David will take care of him, if he is still alive when David becomes king. And if Jonathan isn't alive, he wants David to take care of his descendants. David swears before God that he will keep the covenant," Uncle Jake explained. "And if he doesn't, he calls on God to be his judge. That's *mizpah*."

"So what happened?" Max asked.

"Well, the rest of 1 Samuel talks about Saul chasing David to kill him. What is amazing is that David has an opportunity to kill Saul, but he doesn't out of fear of God and respect for Saul, who was anointed by God to be the first king of Israel. But then Saul and his sons are killed by the Philistines in a battle. Their bodies are hung on the walls at Bet She'an, where we were the other day," Uncle Jake told the kids.

"In the book of 2 Samuel, we're told that one of Saul's sons is still alive. His name is Ish-bosheth. In 2 Samuel 3, we're told the Benjamites, one of the tribes of Israel, wanted Ish-bosheth to be king, so there is a war between the house of David and the house of Saul. In 2 Samuel 4, Ish-bosheth is murdered. David has the murderers put to death because of his covenant with Jonathan.

"David doesn't know there is another descendant of Saul's. Jonathan had a son named Mephibosheth. That's pronounced *meh FIB oh sheth*. Mephibosheth is only five when the report comes that Saul and Jonathan are dead. His nurse takes Mephibosheth, and they run away to hide. In the nurse's hurry, Mephibosheth falls down and injures his legs. After that he can't walk normally."

"That's so sad," Molly said. "Why did the nurse take him and run away?"

"We aren't sure," Uncle Jake answered. "Probably because she was afraid someone would try to kill Mephibosheth since he was related to Saul and Jonathan. Maybe she didn't know there was a covenant between Jonathan and David.

"In 2 Samuel 5, we discover David has been made king of Israel. God makes a covenant with David that his kingdom and throne will endure forever. David defeats the Philistines and conquers the people who were causing Israel trouble. God has taken care of David's enemies.

"But," Uncle Jake said as he stopped and looked at Max and Molly, "what do you think happened to Mephibosheth?"

Max looked at Molly. "I guess that's what we need to find out. Our message told us to go to 2 Samuel 9. Let's talk to God and get started on our hunt for treasure."

Okay, treasure hunter, turn to page 212. Read 2 Samuel 9:1-13 and mark these key words:

David (color it blue)

Ziba (underline it in red)

Mephibosheth (color it orange)

kindness (box it in yellow and color it red, just like you marked *covenant*)

Don't forget to mark the pronouns. And mark anything that tells you WHERE by double underlining the WHERE in green. Mark anything that tells you WHEN by drawing a green clock ⏰ or green circle like this ○.

Make a list on what you learn about Mephibosheth in your field notebook.

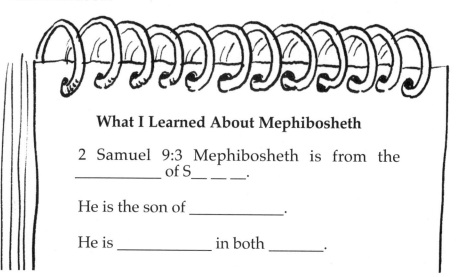

What I Learned About Mephibosheth

2 Samuel 9:3 Mephibosheth is from the _____ of S__ __ __.

He is the son of _____.

He is _____ in both _____.

2 Samuel 9:4 Mephibosheth is living in the house of _____ the _____ of _____ in _____.

2 Samuel 9:6 Mephibosheth came to _____ and fell on his _____ and _____ himself. He told David, "Here is your _____!"

2 Samuel 9:8 Mephibosheth said to David, "What is your _____, that you should _____ a _____ _____ like me?"

2 Samuel 9:9 The king g__ __ __ to Mephibosheth all that _____ to _____ and his house.

2 Samuel 9:11 "Mephibosheth _____ at _____ table as one of the _____ _____."

2 Samuel 9:12 "Mephibosheth had a young _____ whose name was _____."

2 Samuel 9:13 "Mephibosheth lived in _____, for he _____ at the _____ table _____."

Mephibosheth was _____ in both _____.

Isn't that *awesome*? David remembers his covenant with Jonathan. Mephibosheth is living in Lo-debar, a place of bareness. He is crippled and afraid so he is hiding. King David asks if there is anyone left in the house of Saul that he can show kindness to. He finds Mephibosheth, Jonathan's son, and brings him to Jerusalem. David restores his inheritance and gives him a place at his own table. David takes care of Mephibosheth because of his covenant with Jonathan. Isn't that an amazing story of love?

That's what God does for us. We are crippled by sin and run away from God. But God, in His great love for us, sent His Son Jesus Christ to save us. That changes everything! We become children of the King of kings when we accept Jesus as our Lord and Savior. God gives us an inheritance and invites us into His kingdom forever!

Because God loves us, He cut a covenant for us! *What an incredible gift!* Take a few minutes to draw a picture in the box that shows God finding you and inviting you to live in His kingdom, just like David did for Mephibosheth.

Awesome artwork! Don't forget to practice your memory verse.

A BROKEN PROMISE

Today as we continue our hunt for God's treasure, we are going back to the Temple Mount in Jerusalem. We're going to go inside the Western Wall Tunnels. Grab a brochure and let's find out what archeologists have uncovered from Israel's past. Don't forget to ask God for His help.

"Hey look, Molly! You have a code written on your brochure!" Max exclaimed.

"It looks like a zigzag code, Max," Molly responded. "Let's crack the code!"

Okay, treasure hunter, are you ready to crack a zigzag code?

To solve a message written in zigzag code, you put the first word on top and the second word (separated by the dash) on the bottom. Then you space out the letters so they alternate in a zigzag pattern.

Secret Message
2AUL1—SME21:1-14

So you place the letters like this:

2		A		U		L		1-	
	S		M		E		21:		14

Next you take a pen and connect the letters with a zigzag line that goes up and down to each letter. In this instance, you draw a diagonal line from the "2" to the "S." Then you draw a diagonal line from the "S" to the "A." Continue drawing diagonal lines to connect all the letters. Then put the letters in the order they are connected on the following line. The first one is the "2" and the second one is the "S." Decipher the code.

Secret Message Revealed

_____

All right! Now that you have broken the code, turn to page 213, read the passage shown in the secret message, and mark these key words:

God (LORD) (draw a purple triangle and color it yellow)

David (king) (color it blue)

Gibeonites (underline it in brown)

Saul (circle it in black)

Jonathan (color it orange)

famine (box it in black and color it brown)

covenant (oath) (draw a yellow box around it and color it red)

prayer (draw a purple ⌣ and color it pink)

Don't forget to mark the pronouns. And mark anything that tells you WHERE by double underlining the WHERE in green. Mark anything that tells you WHEN by drawing a green clock ⏰ or green circle like this ◯.

Let's hunt for treasure by asking the 5 W's and an H questions.

2 Samuel 21:1 WHY is there a famine in the land?

Because _____ put the _____ to _____

2 Samuel 21:2 WHY was it a problem that Saul killed them? WHAT had the sons of Israel made with the Gibeonites? _____

2 Samuel 21:3 WHAT did David ask the Gibeonites?

"What should I _____ for you? And how can I make _____ that you may _____ the _____ of the _____?"

2 Samuel 21:5-6 WHAT did the Gibeonites want?

_____

_____

2 Samuel 21:6 WHAT did David say?

_____

2 Samuel 21:7 WHO was spared?

_____

WHY? _____

Wow! Can you believe Saul broke the covenant that was made with the Gibeonites? Yes, the Gibeonites deceived the sons of Israel to get them to make this covenant, but that doesn't matter. (You can read about how this covenant was made in Joshua 9.) Remember, covenant is a solemn, binding agreement. When a covenant is made, it is not to be broken. And if it is broken, God is responsible to judge.

Did you see the consequences of the broken covenant? First, there was a famine in the land. And then seven men had to die. Did you notice that Mephibosheth was spared because of David's covenant with Jonathan?

God is the witness and the judge. Making a covenant is serious. It is not to be treated lightly. After David honors his covenant with Jonathan, "God was moved by prayer for the land" (2 Samuel 21:14). Isn't that incredible? What a loving, gracious, and forgiving God we have!

Don't forget to say your memory verse. As you say it, think about what you've learned today about how serious covenant is.

A COVENANT MEAL

"That was so cool!" Max said as they came out of the Western Wall Tunnels. "I loved that secret passage."

"And," Molly added, "getting to touch those ancient stones. I can't believe the wall is still here after so many wars and all those years."

"Think about all the people who have clung to those stones, praying for Messiah to come," Max said. "It's so sad because He came and they didn't recognize Him."

"Why did they miss Jesus as Messiah the first time, Uncle Jake?" Molly asked.

"They expected the Messiah to come as a mighty king to rule the earth. But, instead, Jesus came as a humble man to die for our sins. The next time He comes, it will be to conquer and rule the entire earth!"

"I can't wait!" Max said. "Just think, we get to come with Jesus as a part of His army one day. Jesus will ride in on His white horse, and we'll ride behind him on ours!"

Molly smiled. "And all because of the New Covenant God cut for us. Hey, Uncle Jake, no one has given us a secret message yet. How are we going to find out about covenant today?"

"Let's grab some water and find out."

"You're sneaky, Uncle Jake!" Molly said as she grabbed her bottle of water. "My bottle has a code written on it."

"So does mine," Max chimed in. "Okay, Uncle Jake, how do we crack these codes?"

"Before we crack these codes, we need to take another look at the New Covenant," Uncle Jake said. "Max, why don't you pray for us?"

Take out God's Map, and look up and read Matthew 26:19-32. Then Ask the 5 W's and an H questions.

Matthew 26:19 WHAT feast is being prepared?

_____

Matthew 26:20 WHO is Jesus with?

_____

Matthew 26:26 WHAT happened while they were eating?

_____

_____

Matthew 26:26 WHAT did Jesus say after He blessed and broke the bread?

_____

Matthew 26:27 WHAT did Jesus say after He gave thanks and gave them the cup?

_____

Matthew 26:28 WHAT is this?

_____

WHAT is it poured out for?

_____

As the 12 disciples and Jesus are eating the Passover meal, Jesus did something that wasn't normally done. He asked His disciples to eat the bread that represents His body and drink the wine that represents His blood of the covenant. His blood is going to be poured out to forgive people's sins. This is a picture of Jesus cutting a covenant for us.

Let's find out more! Crack the code written on Molly's water bottle by using the zigzag code, just like you did on Day 4 (page 110).

Zigzag Secret Message
JH6:59—ON53-

Draw diagonal lines to connect all the letters. Then put the letters in the order they are connected on the following line.

J H 6: 59

O N 53-

_____

Now, pull out God's Map and look up those verses. Ask the 5 W's and an H questions.

John 6:53 WHAT *don't* you have if you don't eat Jesus' flesh (the bread) and drink His blood (the wine)?

L__ __ __

John 6:54 WHAT do you have if you take this meal?

_____

John 6:54 WHAT will Jesus do?

_____

John 6:56 WHAT are we doing if we eat His flesh and drink His blood?

We _____ in Jesus and He _____ in us.

In most churches, this "covenant meal" is called the Lord's Supper or Communion. Have you ever eaten the bread (sometimes crackers) and drank the wine (sometimes grape juice) at a Communion Service in church? Did you know that this is a covenant meal? That means you should only eat the bread and drink the wine if you have accepted Jesus Christ as your Savior.

How serious is this covenant meal? Let's find out! Use the zigzag code and solve the mystery message on Max's water bottle.

Zigzag Secret Message
1OITIN11:32—CRNHAS23-

Draw diagonal lines to connect all the letters. Then put the letters in the order they are connected on the following line.

1	O	I	T	I	N	11:	32
	C	R	N	H	A	S	23-

_____

Now turn to page 215. Read the passage in the secret message and mark these key words:

Jesus (Lord) (draw a purple cross and color it yellow)

covenant (draw a yellow box around it and color it red)

judge (judgment) (draw a brown gavel over the word)

For verses 26-32, mark these key words too:

whoever (man, he, you, we) (color it orange)

Now ask the 5 W's and an H questions.

1 Corinthians 11:24-25 WHY are we to eat and drink of the cup?

In _____ of Jesus.

1 Corinthians 11:26 WHAT are we proclaiming?

_____

The reason we take the Lord's Supper or Communion is to remember what Jesus did when He died on the cross. He shed His blood to forgive us of our sins. When we take Communion, we are showing that we are in covenant with Jesus.

1 Corinthians 11:27 HOW can we be "guilty of the body and the blood of the Lord"?

_____

_____

1 Corinthians 11:28 WHAT are we to do?

_____

1 Corinthians 11:29 WHAT are we bringing on ourselves if we do not judge the body rightly? J__ __ __ __ __ __ __

1 Corinthians 11:30 WHAT is that judgment? HOW does God judge those who do not judge the body rightly?

_____

_____

Did you notice the word *sleep*? In this verse, *sleep* means "to die."

> 1 Corinthians 11:31 WHAT happens if we judge ourselves rightly by confessing our sin and stopping what we know is wrong?

> We will not be _____.

Do you see how serious taking the Lord's Supper is? The Lord's Supper (Communion) is a special meal to remember what Jesus Christ did to save us. It would be wrong to know you are sinning, that you are not doing what God says, and take the Lord's Supper. That would be taking the Lord's Supper in an unworthy manner. It is like saying you don't appreciate what God and Jesus did for you.

You are to examine yourself to see if you need to confess any sins in your life *before* eating the bread and drinking the wine (or grape juice) so that you won't be judged and disciplined by God.

> Should you take the Lord's Supper or Communion if you have not accepted Jesus Christ as your Savior?

> _____

> Why or why not? (If you're not sure, read 1 Corinthians 11:29 again.)

> _____

> _____

> Should you play around in church while waiting to take the Lord's Supper? Or should you be thinking about what Jesus Christ did for you? Should you be looking inside your heart to see if you have any sins you need to confess?

> _____

Think about this the next time you are offered the Lord's Supper or Communion at church. This covenant meal is for people who have accepted Jesus Christ as their Savior and have entered into covenant with God through Jesus' shed blood. Do not take eating the bread and drinking the wine (or grape juice) in remembrance of what Jesus did for you lightly. Remember, covenant is serious. Jesus' blood was poured out for the New Covenant to save you!

Now, find a grown-up and say your memory verse out loud to him or her.

Way to go! We are so proud of you!

DYING TO SELF

Last week as we hunted for treasure, we discovered just how serious covenant is and how serious God takes covenant by looking at the covenant term *mizpah. Mizpah* means that God is the One who watches over covenant. He is the witness and the judge. Remember what happened when Saul broke the covenant with the Gibeonites?

We also saw how serious covenant is when we saw how David kept his covenant with Jonathan by taking care of Jonathan's son Mephibosheth. David brought him to his palace in Jerusalem to live with him and eat at his table. That's what God does. He loves us so much that when we enter into covenant with Him, He brings us into His kingdom forever! And that's what we remember when we take the Lord's Supper. The Lord's Supper is not to be taken lightly. It is taken in remembrance of Jesus' death and resurrection.

What will we discover about covenant this week? Let's find out.

THE TREASURE OF BELIEVING GOD

All right, treasure hunter! Pull out your Jerusalem treasure map (page 94) to find out WHERE we are going next. The location is in "K-8." Did you find it? Write out where we are going on the following line.

_____

After we hop into the Jeep, we need to take another look at the covenant God made with Abram. In Week 1, we looked in Genesis 15 at this covenant and the promise that was made. This week we are going to uncover the details.

Don't forget to talk to your Expert Guide.

Okay, turn to page 201. Read Genesis 15:1-6. Ask the 5 W's and an H questions.

Genesis 15:2 WHAT do we learn about Abram?

He is c__ __ __ __ __ __ __ __.

Genesis 15:2-3 WHO does Abram think will be his heir?

_____ of Damascus

Genesis 15:4 WHAT is God's answer?

"This man will not be your _____; but one who will come forth from your _____ _____, he shall be your _____."

Genesis 15:5 WHAT does God tell Abram He will give him?

D__ __ __ __ __ __ __ __ __ __

Did you know that the word translated "descendants" is literally "seed"? Read Galatians 3:16 (page 216).

Galatians 3:16 WHO is the seed God is talking about?

_____

Wow! This is so exciting! Did you know God told Abraham that the Messiah, Jesus Christ, would come from his own bloodline? Isn't that *amazing*?

Now look back at Genesis 15 (page 201).

Genesis 15:6 WHAT was Abram's response?

He _____ in the _____.

Genesis 15:6 WHAT did God do when Abram believed?

"He _____ it to him as

_____."

To be made righteous is to be "made right" with God. How was Abram made right with God? What did Abraham believe? Abraham believed in Jesus Christ—"the seed"—and God declared Abraham as righteous. Jesus said that "Abraham rejoiced to see My day, and he saw it and was glad" (John 8:56). In other words, Abraham believed in Jesus. Abraham believed by faith that Jesus the Messiah was coming, and so Abraham was saved by faith.

Did you know there is only one way that Jews and Gentiles (non-Jews) can be saved? There is only *one* way to salvation no matter who you are. That way is through *faith in Jesus Christ*. Jesus told us, "I am the way, and the truth, and the life; no one comes to the Father but through Me" (John 14:6).

People who were saved *before* Jesus Christ was born were saved because they believed that the Messiah, the promised Savior, would come to fulfill God's promises. They put their trust in Messiah even though He hadn't come to earth as a man yet. Abraham was saved this way.

People who are saved *after* Jesus Christ came to earth are saved because they believe that Jesus is the Messiah, the Son of God. They also believe what the Bible says about Jesus—that He was born of a virgin so He was born without sin, as a man He lived without sinning, and He died to pay for our sins. He was buried, but He was resurrected on the third day. This is the gospel.

Now, before we arrive at the Mount of Olives, you need to grab your compass to decode your memory verse for this week.

Look at the following Compass Code and message. The first blank of each word has a number under it. Find the number on the compass, and then place the letter in that box on the blank.

Next, using that first letter as a starting point, follow the compass directions under the other blanks to find the rest of the letters for that word. To help you get started, we've done the first word for you.

Compass Code

Compass key: N = north or up, S = south or down, E = east or right, W = west or left. NW, SW, SE, NE means you move diagonally.

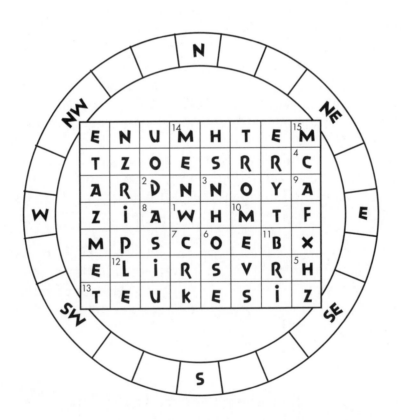

**Compass Secret Message—
This Week's Memory Verse**

W H O E V E R ___ ___ ___ ___ ___ ___ ___ ___ ___ ___
            1 E S E S N SE   2 N E E   3 E SE   4 S NW W SE

___ ___ ___ ___ ___ ___ ___ ___ ___ ___ ___ ___ ___
5 SW W   6 NW N   7 S NE S SE   8 NE W   7 E NE S

___ ___ ___ ___ ___ ___ ___ ___ ___ ___ ___ ___ ___ ___ ___
9 S W SW SE   10 S   7 NW NE E E SE   11 W   10 NE

___ ___ ___ ___ ___ ___ ___ ___ ___ ___ 14:27
2 SW SE E SW NW S S   12 SE E E

You did it! Now, write this verse out on an index card and practice saying it three times in a row, three times today.

Tomorrow we'll find out what happens after Abraham believed God.

DAY TWO

GOD CUTS COVENANT

"Wow, this is so cool, Uncle Jake!" Max said as he looked around on the Mount of Olives. "I can't believe we are standing on the mountain where Jesus taught His disciples! It's also where He ascended into heaven 40 days after His resurrection."

"And," Molly added, "this is the mountain that Jesus

will someday return to, and it will split in two like the prophet Zechariah says."

Uncle Jake smiled. "Good job, Max and Molly. Let's sit down and pick up where we left off yesterday. We read that God told Abram that Jesus Christ would come from his seed."

"And," Max jumped in, "Abram believed God. Abram got saved!"

"So what happened after Abram believed?" Uncle Jake asked. "Molly, why don't you pray, and then we can get to work."

All right! Now that we have prayed, turn to page 201. Read Genesis 15:7-18, and ask the 5 W's and an H questions. You probably will remember this from Week 1, Day 5, when we discovered that Abram cut the animals in two.

Genesis 15:12 WHAT happened after the animals were cut?

_____

Genesis 15:17 WHAT happened after the sun set?

"There appeared a _____ _____ and

a _____ _____ which _____

between these _____."

WHO is this smoking oven and flaming torch that

passes through the pieces?

_____

Genesis 15:18 WHAT did God do?

"The LORD m__ __ __ a __ __ __ __ __ __ __ __ __ with

__ __ __ __ __."

The Hebrew word for *made* is *karath,* which means "to cut." The Hebrew word for *covenant* is *beriyth.* It is a compact or agreement made by passing through pieces of flesh.

In covenant, after the pieces of the sacrificed animal were cut and laid opposite each other, the people making the covenant would walk between the pieces of the animal. This symbolized a "walk into death." What does this "walk into death" mean? When you make a covenant, you are saying you won't put yourself first anymore. You are "dying to self" and putting your covenant partner ahead of what you want or need. You "die to what you want to do and how you want to live." Instead, you choose to live for your covenant partner.

> Genesis 15:18 WHAT was the promise made in this covenant?
>
> "To your _____ I have given this _____."
>
> Were there any conditions to the covenant? _____
>
> Genesis 15:17-18 WHO made the agreement? WHO passed through or between the pieces of flesh?
>
> _____

That makes this an *unconditional* covenant. Abram was asleep, so he didn't do anything. God is the one who passed through the pieces of flesh as a smoking oven and a flaming torch.

So do we ever walk through pieces of flesh? Do we to take a "walk into death" by dying to our wants and needs to put someone else first? We'll find out as we continue to uncover God's treasure.

Don't forget to practice your memory verse!

THE MYSTERY OF THE VEIL

"Sam, come back here!" Max yelled.

Sam ran around in circles barking at Max and Molly as they tried to catch him. Sam dodged out of Molly's reach and ran straight into Uncle Jake.

"Gotcha!" Uncle Jake exclaimed and then smiled. "Okay, boy. That's enough. Sit. Now leave it." Sam obediently sat down, lowered his head, and released the paper that was in his mouth. "I think Sam wanted to be the first one to find out where we're headed next!"

"You are such a bad dog, Sam!" Max scolded as Molly looked at the message.

Molly said, "It's a bit wet, but I can read it."

Here's the message for you to decode using the compass on page 124, treasure hunter!

Compass Secret Message

___ ___ ___ ___ ___   ___ ___ ___ ___ ___
13 N   N   E   S   S   14 SW   N   W   SW

All right! Let's pile into the Jeep and talk to God.

Yesterday we saw God cut a covenant with Abram by walking through the pieces of animal flesh (the sacrifice) as a smoking oven and a flaming torch. Today we're going to head back to the Temple Mount to take a closer look at what Jesus did for us.

Pull out God's Map, and look up and read Mark 15:25 and 33-39.

Mark 15:25 WHAT is happening to Jesus?

He is being _____.

Mark 15:25 WHEN is this happening?

The _____ _____

Mark 15:33 WHAT happened in the sixth hour?

"_____ fell over the whole _____."

Mark 15:34 WHAT happened in the ninth hour?

"Jesus _____ _____ with a loud voice, *'Eloi,*
Eloi, Lama Sabachthani.' "

Mark 15:35 WHAT did these words spoken in Aramaic
mean?

"My _____, My _____, why have You
_____ Me?"

Mark 15:37 WHAT happened?

"Jesus uttered a _____ _____, and
_____ His last."

Mark 15:38 WHAT happened next?

"The _____ of the _____ was _____ in
_____ from _____ to _____."

Draw a picture of this amazing event in the box.

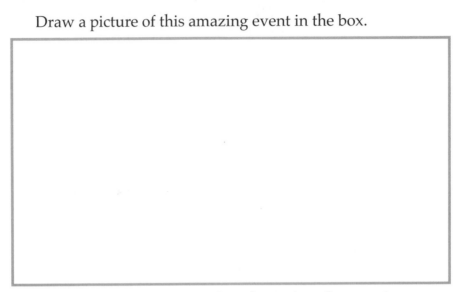

Fantastic! Did you know that the veil in the temple was so thick and heavy it would have taken two teams of horses pulling in opposite directions to tear it in two? Do you know what the veil is a picture of? If you're not sure, hang in here with us. You'll find out soon!

Don't forget to practice your memory verse!

ENTERING INTO GOD'S PRESENCE

"Okay, guys," Uncle Jake said, "let's sit on the old stone steps that lead up to the Temple Mount."

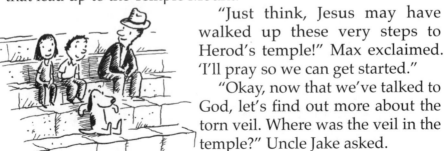

"Just think, Jesus may have walked up these very steps to Herod's temple!" Max exclaimed. 'I'll pray so we can get started."

"Okay, now that we've talked to God, let's find out more about the torn veil. Where was the veil in the temple?" Uncle Jake asked.

"I know," Molly answered. "The veil separated the holy place, where the lampstand, the table of showbread, and the altar of incense was, from the holy of holies, where the ark of the covenant was."

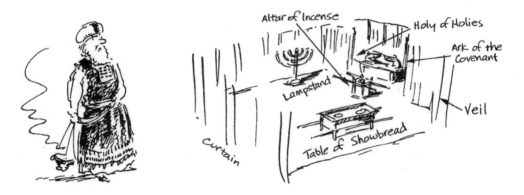

"And," Max added, "Each one of those pieces of furniture showed a picture of Jesus. For instance, the lampstand was a picture that Jesus is the light. And the showbread was a picture that Jesus is the bread of life."

Molly jumped in, "And on the altar of incense, incense was burned daily to show that Jesus is our High Priest who intercedes for us with God. That means Jesus prays for us. He goes to God on our behalf."

"Great, you two!" Uncle Jake smiled. "What was behind the veil inside the holy of holies?"

Max answered, "The ark of the covenant, which is a picture of the throne of God. Once a year the high priest entered the holy of holies to sprinkle blood on the 'mercy seat' on the ark of the covenant for the Jewish people's sins. When the high priest entered the holy of holies, he was entering into the presence of God."

"All right! So..." Uncle Jake paused for a second. "What is the torn veil a picture of?"

Okay, treasure hunter. Let's find out about the mystery of the torn veil in the temple. Turn to page 218. Read Hebrews 10:19-20 and mark these key words:

Jesus (draw a purple cross and color it yellow)

blood (draw three dots of blood)

veil (box it in purple and put a red tear down the middle like this: ᶘ)

Don't forget to mark the pronouns!
Discover the treasure by asking the 5 W's and an H questions.

Hebrews 10:19 HOW can we have confidence to enter the holy place?

_____

Hebrews 10:20 WHAT is the veil?

Jesus' _____

Pull out God's Map. Look up and read Mark 15:33-38 again.

Mark 15:37 WHAT did Jesus do before He breathed His last breath?

"Jesus uttered a _____ _____."

Look up and read John 19:30 in God's Map. WHAT did Jesus say just before He died?

"_____ _____ _____!"

Did you know when Jesus cried out "It is finished" on the cross, He was saying that He had paid for our sins in full?
Now look back at Mark 15:37-38 in God's Map.

Mark 15:38 WHAT happened after Jesus uttered his loud cry and died?

_____

Look up and read John 14:6 in God's Map.

John 14:6 WHAT do we see about Jesus?

Jesus said, "I am the _____, and the _____,

and the _____; no _____ comes to the _____

but through ____."

WHO is the *only* way to get into the presence of God?

_____

Isn't it amazing that when Jesus died God ripped the temple veil in two? The veil was a symbol of Jesus' flesh. When Jesus shed His blood, an offering was made for sin once and for all so that we can come into the presence of God. To enter into covenant with God, we have to come through the veil. And God has told us that Jesus is the veil. So Jesus is the *only* way to God. There is no other way!

You are doing great! Now let's find out where we're going next. Turn to the treasure map of Jerusalem (page 94). Write down the next location by finding "K-7" and "K-6" on the map.

G__ __ __ __ __ __ __ __ and the

C__ __ __ __ __ of __ __ __ N__ __ __ __ __

Don't forget to practice saying your memory verse.

THE COST TO FOLLOW JESUS

"Look at the dome and starlike lights!" Molly exclaimed as they walked inside the Church of All Nations on the Mount of Olives.

"That's to create a somber mood and remind us of the sorrow Jesus felt when He prayed that night in the Garden of Gethsemane," Uncle Jake explained. He pointed to a huge rock in front of the main altar. "That is the 'rock of agony,' where some people believe Jesus prayed 'yet not My will, but Yours be done' when He was praying about dying on the cross before He was arrested."

"Look at that huge crown of thorns that surrounds the rock. May we walk around the rock, Uncle Jake?"

"Sure you can. As you do, think about what it cost Jesus to enter into covenant with you. Then we'll go outside and find a place to sit in the Garden of Gethsemane and find out if there is a cost for us to enter into God's New Covenant."

All right, treasure hunter, stop and think about what Jesus told God in the Garden of Gethsemane. He said He wanted God's will to be done instead of His. Jesus was willing to die on a cross for us. So WHAT does it cost us to be in covenant with Jesus? WHAT is the cost of following Jesus and becoming His disciples? Talk to God, and then we'll find out.

Turn to page 219. Read Luke 14:25-33 and mark the following key words:

Jesus (He, Him, Me, and My) (draw a purple cross and color it yellow)

the people (crowds, them, anyone, he, his, disciple) (color it orange)

✝ cross (draw a red cross)

Ask the 5 W's and an H questions to uncover the cost of the treasure.

Luke 14:26 HOW do you come to Jesus? HOW can you be Jesus' disciple?

You must h__ __ __ your _____ and _____

and _____ and _____ and _____ and

_____, and even your own _____.

Does Jesus mean we have to literally hate our families? No. He is telling us that we are to put Him first. That we are not to put anyone before Him. Jesus is to have *first place* in our lives. He is to be loved above all others.

Luke 14:27 HOW are we to be Jesus' disciples?

Carry our own _____ and follow _____.

Did you know that the cross represents death? To follow Jesus by taking up our cross means we must die to self. This is what Jesus was doing when He said to God in the Garden of Gethsemane, "Not My will, but Yours be done."

Jesus died so we could enter into God's presence. We are to

die to self by giving up our rights and doing what God wants us to do instead of what we want to do. That means there will be a complete change in the way we live when we accept Jesus as our Savior. Jesus now has first place. We die to ourselves and live for Him!

Read Luke 14:28-32 (page 219). Look at the examples Jesus gives about following Him—building a tower, laying a foundation, and going to battle.

Luke 14:28 WHAT are we to calculate before we get

started? The _____

God gives us the *gift* of salvation. We can't earn salvation. But salvation cost Jesus His life. And when we enter into covenant with Him, there is a cost for us too. We have to die to ourselves and start living for God. WHAT are some of other costs to following Jesus?

Read Luke 14:33. HOW do you become Jesus' disciple?

_____ _____ all my _____.

You have to be willing to give up *everything* for Jesus. To discover some more costs of being a disciple of Jesus, get out God's Map and look up and read these verses from Matthew 10. Fill in the blanks by unscrambling the mixed up words.

Matthew 10:17 You may be handed over to the _____ (ourtsc).

Matthew 10:21 You may be _____ (etrbayed) by family.

Matthew 10:22 You will be _____ (athed) because of Jesus' name.

Matthew 10:23 You will be _____ (erespctdeu).

Matthew 10:32 You are to _____ (oncessf) Jesus before men.

Matthew 10:37 You are not to _____ (ovel) anyone more than Jesus.

Matthew 10:28 You must take up your _____ roscs) and _____ (olfowl) Jesus.

Matthew 10:39 You are to be willing to _____ (olse) your _____ (ifel) for Jesus' sake.

Now look up and read Philippians 1:29 in God's Map.

Philippians 1:29 WHAT have you been granted?

To _____ in Christ and to _____ for His sake

We have been granted to *believe in Jesus Christ,* but we have also been granted to *suffer for His sake.* Did you know that? Everyone wants the good parts of being a Christian, but we see there are some hard parts to being a Christian too.

To be Jesus' disciple, you must be willing to suffer for Him. People may hate you because you love Jesus. They may judge you, make fun of you, betray you, hurt you, turn their backs on you, and even take your life. What should you do when you go through these things? Let's find out by reading Matthew 10:22 again.

> Matthew 10:22 Jesus said, "You will be hated by all because of My name, but it is the one who has endured to the end who will be saved."

WHAT are you to do to the end?

_____

That's the cost of following Jesus. Even if you are hated, you are to endure to the end. Are you willing to pay the cost to follow Jesus? Think about it carefully. Jesus gave His life for you. That's why you have to be willing to choose to do what Jesus says instead of what your friends want you to do. You have to let Jesus have first place. You have to give Jesus Christ *everything*.

Don't forget to say your memory verse out loud to a grown-up. Ask them if they have died to themselves to be Jesus' disciple.

COVENANT OF LAW

How do you like being a treasure hunter so far? Pretty cool, isn't it? You uncovered a very big find last week when you discovered salvation is a gift from God. You can't earn salvation, but you have to die to yourself to receive it. Jesus gave His life to save you, and you need to be willing to put Jesus first and to suffer for Him. You have to give Jesus everything. There is a cost to following Jesus, but you also get to live with Him forever!

This week as we continue our quest for God's treasure, we need to take another look at God's Covenant of Law (the "Old Covenant") to discover WHY God gave this covenant and how the covenant with Abraham (the Abrahamic covenant), the Old Covenant, and the New Covenant fit together to bring us to salvation. Grab your maps, and keep up the great work!

DAY ONE

GOD GIVES THE LAW

"Look, Max! Sam has something in his mouth," Molly said as she noticed Sam sitting behind a bush.

"He sure does. Come here, boy!" Max said. "Leave it, Sam," Max said

after Sam came. When Sam dropped the paper, Max said, "Good boy!" and patted his pup's head. "Hey, Uncle Jake, did you put Sam up to this?"

"Who me?" Uncle Jake smiled. "You did great, Sam, old boy. Okay, you two, crack today's secret code."

Here's the secret message, treasure hunter. Start on the far right, and write each letter from right to left on the lines.

Secret Message

wal   fo   tnanevoc

_____   _____   _____

Great! Now talk to God, and then we'll take another look at the covenant in the secret message.

Turn to page 205. Read Exodus 19:1-6 and answer the 5 W's and an H questions.

Exodus 19:1 WHERE are "the sons of Israel"?

_____

Exodus 19:1 WHERE did they come from?

_____

Exodus 19:2 WHERE are they camped?

_____

Exodus 19:3 WHAT did Moses do?

_____

Exodus 19:5 WHAT did God tell him to do?

_____

Exodus 19:5-6 WHAT will the people be if they obey and keep the covenant?

_____

Pull out God's Map. Look up and read Exodus 20:1-18.

Exodus 20:1 WHAT is God doing?

_____

Do you know what these words are? They are the Ten Commandments. This is the "Covenant of Law," also known as the "Old Covenant."

Are you ready to find out your memory verse for this week? Then you get to decode another secret message! Start with the first line on the far right. Write the letters from right to left on the lines. Do the same thing for each line.

Secret Message

eht ni ti daer dna tnanevoc eht fo koob eht koot eh nehT

sah DROL eht taht llA" ,dias yeht dna ;elpoep eht fo gniraeh

"!tneidebo eb lliw ew dna ,od lliw ew nekops

7:42 sudoxE

Memory Verse Decoded

_____

_____

_____

_____

_____

_____ 24:7

Great work! Practice saying this verse out loud, three times in a row, three times today.

THE BOOK OF THE COVENANT

Good morning! Are you ready to head out on our next adventure? Pull out your treasure map of Jerusalem (page 94) to find out where we're going next. Look at "F-6," and write down our next location.

_____

All right! Now hop into the Jeep. Let's find out more about the Covenant of Law while we head back to the Old City in Jerusalem. Don't forget to pray!

Yesterday in Exodus 19 and 20, we discovered that *after* the sons of Israel are rescued from the land of Egypt, they camp in the wilderness at Sinai. Moses goes up to God on the mountain, and God gives Moses the Covenant of Law, which is the Ten Commandments. In Exodus chapters 20 through 23, God gives Moses the ordinances (other laws) to set before the sons of Israel.

So, how is the Covenant of Law similar and different from the other covenants we've studied? WHY did God give the Covenant of Law? Let's find out. Turn to page 205. Read Exodus 24:3-12. Ask the 5 W's and an H questions.

Exodus 24:4 WHAT did Moses do?

"Moses _____ down _____ the _____ of the _____."

Exodus 24:7 WHAT did Moses do with the book of the covenant?

_____

Exodus 24:7 HOW did the people respond? WHAT did they promise?

"All that the _____ has spoken, we will _____,

and we will be _____!"

Do you see how this covenant is different from the covenant God made with Abraham (the Abrahamic covenant)? Abraham didn't do anything for that covenant. But in the Covenant of Law, the people *promise* to keep the covenant. This is a *two-way, conditional* covenant.

WHAT things do you see in the Covenant of Law that are similar to other covenants we've looked at?

Exodus 24:8 WHAT did Moses sprinkle on the people?

_____

Have we seen blood in the other covenants? _____

Exodus 24:11 WHAT did the sons of the nobles of Israel do when they saw God? _____

Does this remind you of the covenant meal?

_____ Yes   _____ No

Exodus 24:12 WHAT did God say He was going to give Moses?

_____

Exodus 24:12 WHY did God write the law and the commandment?

_____

God gave the Ten Commandments to the sons of Israel because they had been living in bondage in Egypt, and now that they are out of bondage, God wanted them to know how to live and worship Him in the land of Canaan. God gave them instructions to teach them what is right and wrong so they would know what they should and shouldn't do.

Since the Law—the Old Covenant—came *after* the Abrahamic Covenant, does the Old Covenant replace the Abrahamic Covenant? We'll find out tomorrow!

Don't forget to practice your memory verse.

DAY THREE

GOD'S PROMISE

"Wow, I love the Old City!" Molly said as they wandered through the streets.

"Did you know that the Old City is divided into four neighborhoods called quarters, which are named according to the groups of people who live in them?" Uncle Jake asked.

"Are the quarters called the Christian Quarter, the Armenian Quarter, the Muslim Quarter, and the Jewish Quarter?" Max asked.

"That's right, Max," Uncle Jake answered. "Let's head into

the Jewish Quarter and have a bagel at a cafe while we discover how the Abrahamic Covenant and the Covenant of Law (Old Covenant) relate to each other."

Don't forget to talk to God, treasure hunter! Then turn to page 216. Read Galatians 3:15-18 and ask the 5 W's and an H questions.

Galatians 3:16 WHO were the promises spoken to?

_____

Galatians 3:16 WHO is the seed? _____

Galatians 3:17 WHEN did the Law come?

_____

Galatians 3:17 Does the Covenant of Law take the place of the promise God made to Abraham?

_____ Yes _____ No

Galatians 3:17 HOW do you know? WHAT does it say?

_____

Galatians 3:18 WHAT is the inheritance based on?

_____

Isn't that *awesome*? The Covenant of Law *does not take away* (replace) the Abrahamic Covenant because the Abrahamic covenant was granted to Abraham by God's promise! The Law cannot invalidate (make void) a covenant confirmed by God. In the Abrahamic Covenant, God promises Abraham descendants (the "seed," who is Jesus) and land. Jesus Christ will come from Abraham's descendants.

Since God has promised the seed (Jesus), WHY did He give the Law? In Exodus 24, we discovered the Covenant of Law was given to *help* the sons of Israel. It was for their instruction. Tomorrow we will get more details on why the Law was added. Hang in here. You are doing great! Don't forget to practice your memory verse.

THE TUTOR

"That was fun wandering through the Jewish Quarter, Uncle Jake," Molly said. "Where are we going next?"

Uncle Jake smiled. "We are going to Misgav Ladach Street to visit a very special place—the Temple Institute (in Hebrew it's called the Machon HaMikdash). The Temple Institute is a nonprofit, Jewish organization dedicated to educating people about the Holy Temple the Jews believe they are to build in preparation for the coming of the Messiah."

"Wow, that sounds cool!" Max exclaimed.

Sam barked his agreement.

"You're going to love it. But before we visit, we need to find out more about why God gave the Covenant of Law. Let's get a cool drink and sit over there to study. Molly, why don't you pray for us so we can get started?"

"You got it, Uncle Jake," Molly said.

Now that we've prayed, let's turn to page 217. Read Galatians 3:19-25. Ask the 5 W's and an H questions.

> Galatians 3:19 WHAT was the Law for? WHY was it added?
>
> It was added because of _____ until the
>
> _____ would come.

Galatians 3:24 WHAT is the Law?

_____

Galatians 3:24-25 Do we need the tutor now that Christ has come?

_____

Look back at Galatians 3:10. WHAT is "everyone who does not abide by all things written in the book of the Law, to perform them"?

_____

Pull out God's map, the Bible, and read Romans 7:7. HOW do we know about sin? Through the _____

God gave the Law to be our "tutor" (our teacher) to show us our sins. How could we know what sin is if God didn't show us what was right and wrong by giving us His Law?

Did you know that in order to keep the Law—the commandments—a person had to keep *all* of them, not just the parts he liked? If he broke one law, he broke them all. And because we are born sinners, people can't keep all the law no matter how hard we try. That's why Jesus came to bring the New Covenant!

Does the New Covenant replace the Old Covenant? You'll find out next week!

Practice your memory verse. We are so proud of you!

WORSHIPPING UNDER THE LAW

"Wow, look at that!" Molly exclaimed. "That's a menorah—a 7-branched candlestick."

"I didn't picture it being so big. Is it made with real gold, Uncle Jake?" Max asked.

"It sure is," Uncle Jake answered. "The reason I wanted you to visit the Temple Institute is because after God made the Covenant of Law with the sons of Israel, He had them build a tabernacle where they could worship Him. Since we are going to find out how God told the sons of Israel to worship Him today, I thought you would like to see the actual vessels and items that will be used inside when the third temple will be built. The vessels we are looking at are authentic, accurate vessels, not just replicas or models. They are built according to the exact specifications given in the Bible."

"That's incredible!" Molly exclaimed. "I can't believe we are looking at the menorah this Jewish group believes will be used when the temple is rebuilt in Jerusalem."

"It sure is," Uncle Jake stated. "Are you ready to find out how God told Moses and the sons of Israel to worship Him?"

"We sure are!" Max and Molly agreed.

Sam barked and wagged his tail.

All right, treasure hunter, we need to find out WHAT God tells the sons of Israel to do to worship Him after He gives them the Covenant of Law. To "worship" is to "bow before God and honor Him for who He is."

Don't forget to pray! Then pull out God's Map. Look up and read Exodus 25.

Exodus 25:8 WHY are they to construct a sanctuary for God?

_____

Exodus 25:9 HOW are they to construct this sanctuary?

_____

Exodus 25:10 WHAT are they to construct?

_____

Exodus 25:21 WHAT are they to put on top of the ark?

_____

Exodus 25:18 WHAT goes at each end of the mercy seat?

_____

Exodus 25:21-22 WHERE will God meet with them?

"Above the _____ _____, from between the

_____ _____ which are upon the _____ of

the _____."

Exodus 25:22 WHAT will God do?

_____

_____

Isn't that *incredible*? God said He would meet with them inside the tabernacle they were to build to worship Him. God gives them a plan, or pattern, to show them exactly what to build.

Do you remember that each piece of the furniture inside the tabernacle represents Jesus? (If you don't, go back and read the information in Week 5, Day 4.)

Look at the following drawing of the Tabernacle or make your own tabernacle like Max and Molly did. (To make a tabernacle like Max and Molly get a shoebox, scissors, a marking pen for writing, a brown marking pen, a blue marking pen, a red marking pen, and a purple marking pen, a stapler, and two handkerchiefs (or one brown piece of cloth and one blue, red, and purple cloth) big enough to go across the narrow part of the shoebox. We'll provide instructions as we go along. As you make your tabernacle or look at our drawing, think about each piece of furniture and what it represents.)

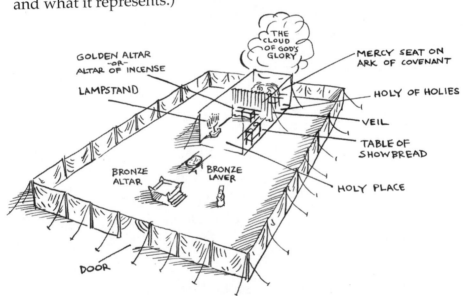

There is a gate into the outer court. (Cut an opening at one end of the shoebox to create a "gate" into the outer court.)

The bronze altar was where the people brought offerings to the Lord. Bronze is a symbol of judgment. The animals to be sacrificed were tied to the four horns or ends, one on each corner. This is a picture of Jesus as the Lamb of God who was sacrificed to take away the sins of the world. (Draw a picture of the bronze altar on the "floor" of the shoebox just after you "come through the gate.")

Next comes the bronze laver. This is where the priests washed daily. Jesus is the Word, and the Word makes us clean (John 15:3). (Draw a picture of the bronze laver after you've "gone through the gate and passed the bronze altar.")

Then we come to a curtain. This curtain is the only door into the holy place of the tabernacle. This door faces east. Jesus is the door (John 10:9). He is the *only* way people can come to God. (Take your handkerchief and color it brown. Cut a slit in the middle for the entrance. Use a stapler to hang it as a curtain that separates the outer part of the tabernacle from the "holy place.")

When you enter through the curtain, this is called the holy place. On the left is a lampstand—a 7-branch candlestick made of pure gold. It used olive oil and was kept lit day and night. It was the only light inside the tabernacle. Jesus is the light (John 1:4)! (Draw a lampstand on the left, just inside the curtain).

Next let's look at the table of showbread. It sits on the right, across from the lampstand. On it were 12 loaves of bread. Every Jewish Sabbath (Saturday), the loaves of bread were eaten by the priests and fresh bread was placed on the table. Jesus is the bread of life (John 6:48)!

After the lampstand and table of showbread comes the altar of incense, placed in the middle of the holy place. Incense was burned continually to show Jesus is our High Priest who lives to make intercession for us! Intercession means that Jesus prays for us. Jesus goes to God on our behalf (Hebrews 7:25).

Next, we come to the temple veil. It hangs right behind the altar of incense. The veil separated the holy place from the holy of holies. The only way into the holy of holies was through the veil. Remember what we learned about the torn veil inside the temple? It was ripped in two when Jesus died on the cross. The veil is a picture of J__ __ __ __' f__ __ __ __. To get to the throne of God, we have to go through Jesus (Hebrews 10:20). (Take the second handkerchief and color it blue, red, and purple to represent the veil in the tabernacle. Cut a slit in the middle for the entrance. Hang it right behind the altar of incense.)

Behind the veil is the holy of holies. Only the high priest could enter this area to sprinkle blood on the mercy seat for his sins and the Jewish people's sins. Inside the ark of the covenant were the tablets of stone (the Ten Commandments), a pot of manna (the bread God fed the sons of Israel in the wilderness), and Aaron's rod that budded. This is a picture of the throne of God. Jesus' blood was shed as a sacrifice to pay for our sins so that through Him (the torn veil) we can enter into the presence of God.

Isn't God *awesome*! Why don't you take a few minutes to think about the treasure you've discovered and worship God by praising Him for who He is? Or you can sing a song of praise for what He did for you!

After that, hop into the Jeep and find our next location. Pull out your Jerusalem treasure map (page 94). Locate "I-2" and write down our next location.

_____

Way to go! You have done an amazing job! Don't forget to practice your memory verse.

COVENANTS OF SALVATION

Wasn't it exciting exploring the Old City in Jerusalem last week as we took another look at God's Covenant of Law? We discovered that the Covenant of Law *did not replace* the Abrahamic covenant (God's promise of the seed, Jesus Christ, and land). God gave the Covenant of Law to be our "tutor" to show us our sins.

We also saw how God gave the pattern of the tabernacle so the sons of Israel could worship Him. Wasn't it cool to see how each piece of furniture in the tabernacle represented Jesus and how we can enter God's presence?

But don't stop yet! This week we get to uncover more details about God's covenants of salvation.

ANOTHER COVENANT

"Look, Molly!" Max exclaimed. "We're in the city of David. Hey, Uncle Jake, I have a feeling that coming here is a clue to discovering our next covenant."

"You're right, Max! You have me all figured out. So what does this clue tell us about our next covenant?"

"I know," Molly spoke up. "I bet this covenant has to do with David."

"That's a good guess, Molly. Have you ever heard Jesus called the 'son of David'? Or that Jesus was born of the tribe of Judah in the family of David?"

"I have, Uncle Jake," Max answered.

"So," Uncle Jake said, "we're going to find out how important that information is!"

Okay, treasure hunter, crack the following code to find out the next covenant. Start on the far right and write each letter from right to left on the lines below the code.

Secret Message

tnanevoC   cidivaD

_____   _____

Now, ask for God's help and then get out His Map, the Bible. Look up and read Psalm 89:3-4.

Psalm 89:3 WHAT did God make with David?

_____

Psalm 89:4 WHAT will God establish?

_____

Remember, "seed" is descendants. Psalm 89:4 For HOW long will this be established?

_____

Now, let's see when God made this covenant in David's life. Turn to page 219 and read 2 Samuel 7:1-18. Mark these key words:

God (the LORD) (draw a purple triangle and color it yellow)

David (color it blue)

house (but only when it's a house for God) (box it in blue)

Don't forget to mark the pronouns. And mark anything that tells you WHEN by drawing a green clock or green circle like this ◯ . Ask the 5 W's and an H questions.

2 Samuel 7:1-5 WHAT does David want to do for the LORD?

B__ __ __ __   God a _____ to _____ in

2 Samuel 7:6 WHERE had God been dwelling?

_____

2 Samuel 7:8 WHAT did God do for David?

God made David _____ over His people _____

2 Samuel 7:9 WHERE has God been?

God has been _____ David wherever he has gone.

2 Samuel 7:9 WHAT has God done?

God c__ __   __ __ __ all David's _____.

2 Samuel 7:9 WHAT is God going to do?

God will make David a great _____.

2 Samuel 7:11 WHAT else is God going to do?

The LORD will make a _____ for David.

2 Samuel 7:12 WHAT will God do after David dies?

God will raise up David's _____.

2 Samuel 7:16 HOW long will David's house last?

David's _____ and his _____ shall

_____ before God _____. David's _____

will be established _____.

2 Samuel 7:12-13 WHO will build God's house for Him?

_____

Even though the word *covenant* isn't used in 2 Samuel 7, by also looking at Psalm 89, we see that God is making a covenant with David and his descendants (his seed) forever.

Now, look up Matthew 1:1-2 in God's Map.

Matthew 1:1-2 WHO is Jesus?

The son of _____, the son of _____

In God's Map, look up and read Acts 13:16-34.

Acts 13:22 WHO did God raise up to be king?

_____

Acts 13:23 WHO has God brought from David's descendants to Israel?

_____

Acts 13:26 WHAT is the message the apostle Paul is talking about?

_____

Acts 13:33 WHAT did God do?

_____

Acts 13:33 HOW did He fulfill the promise?

_____

How cool is that? God promises the "seed"—Jesus Christ—through the Abrahamic and Davidic Covenants.

Okay, let's discover this week's memory verse. Look at the hearts below. Inside each heart is a word that has been mixed up. Crack the code for this week's verse by unscrambling each word inside a heart and then writing them in order on the blanks on the next page.

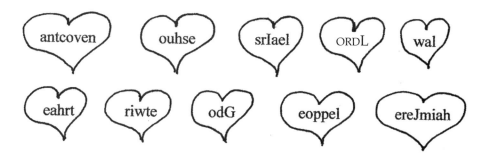

antcoven   ouhse   srIael   ORDL   wal

eahrt   riwte   odG   eoppel   ereJmiah

"But this is the _____ which I will make with the

_____ of _____ after those days," declares

the _____, "I will put My _____ within them and

on their _____ I will _____ it; and I will be

their _____, and they shall be My _____."

_____ 31:33

Fantastic! Now, write this verse out on an index card and practice saying it out loud three times in a row, three times today.

WHAT is this covenant God will write on the house of Israel's hearts? Do you know? You'll find out this week!

A BROKEN COVENANT

"Okay, guys," Uncle Jake said. "Let's go sit in the courtyard and uncover more of God's treasure."

"That's a great idea," Molly said. "I'll pray so we can get started."

After they prayed, Uncle Jake said, "Yesterday when we studied the Davidic Covenant, we saw God tell David that his descendant would build a house of worship. That descendant was David's son King Solomon. King Solomon built God a magnificent temple, but as he grew old, he turned his heart away from God and toward other gods. So God tore the kingdom from Solomon's hands and gave part of it to his servant. From that point on, the 12 tribes of Israel were divided into two kingdoms: the Northern Kingdom and the Southern Kingdom. The Northern Kingdom of Israel was made up of 10 tribes, and the Southern Kingdom of Judah was made up of 2 tribes, Benjamin and Judah."

Uncle Jake continued. "In 722 BC, the Northern Kingdom of Israel is conquered and the people go into captivity under the Assyrians. Even though the Southern Kingdom of Judah sees the Northern Kingdom of Israel go into captivity, the people don't stop sinning against God. So God sends His prophet Jeremiah to warn the Southern Kingdom of Judah."

Okay, treasure hunter, let's find out WHAT God tells Jeremiah to say.

Turn to page 221. Read Jeremiah 11:1-11 and mark this key word:

covenant (oath) (draw a yellow box around it and color it red)

Uncover God's treasure by asking the 5 W's and an H questions.

Jeremiah 11:10 WHAT does God say the house of Israel and the house of Judah did?

"They have b__ __ __ __ __   My _____."

Jeremiah 11:10 HOW did they do that?

_____

_____

WHAT covenant did they break? Remember what you learned in Exodus 20 and 24. WHAT is the name of this covenant?

_____

Jeremiah 11:11 WHAT are the consequences of breaking this covenant? WHAT will God do?

_____

_____

How sad! Israel and Judah have broken the Covenant of Law (the Old Covenant). They did not obey or listen to God. They have walked in the stubbornness of their evil hearts. They have served other gods, and now the one true God is going to bring disaster on them. Israel and Judah's sin has broken God's heart. Is there any hope? We'll find out tomorrow.

Don't forget to practice your memory verse. Here's a hint to think about: Your memory verse is a clue about WHAT God is going to do for His people.

THE NEW COVENANT

Good morning! Are you ready to head out on our next adventure? Pull out your Jerusalem treasure map (page 94) to find out WHERE we are going next. Look for "H-1," and write down our next location.

_____

As we head to our new destination, we need to find out if there is any hope for God's people now that they have broken the Covenant of Law. Talk to God. Then turn to page 221. Read Jeremiah 31:31-34 and mark these key words:

covenant (draw a yellow box around it and color it red)

law (draw black tablets)

heart (draw a red heart)

Now, hunt for the treasure by asking the 5 W's and an H questions.

Jeremiah 31:31 WHAT is God going to make with the house of Israel and the house of Judah?

_____

WHAT was the covenant God made with their fathers when He brought them out of Israel?

_____

WHERE did God write the Old Covenant?

_____

Jeremiah 31:33 WHAT is different about this New Covenant? WHERE will God write it?

_____

Jeremiah 31:34 WHAT will the Lord do?

_____

_____

Wow! The sons of Israel broke God's Old Covenant, which brings disaster on them. But what will God do? He is going to make a New Covenant with them. This time instead of writing it on stone tablets, He will put it inside them. He will write it on their hearts. And He will forgive their iniquity and remember their sins no more. What an *awesome* God!

WHAT is this New Covenant God will write on their hearts? Grab God's Map. Look up and read Matthew 26:26-29. WHOSE blood is poured out for the forgiveness of sins?

_____

Jesus dying on the cross to save us is the New Covenant! The Old Covenant has been broken, so God provides a New Covenant. God loves us so much that He provides a message of hope, saying He will forgive our sins through Jesus Christ and remember them no more!

Fill in the following chart to compare the Old and New Covenants. After you fill in the blanks, draw a picture of each covenant that shows where God writes the law for each covenant.

Old Covenant (The Law)	New Covenant
Exodus 24:12 The Old Covenant was written on s___ ___ ___e t___ ___ ___ ___ ___s	**Jeremiah 31:33** I will put My _____ _____ them and on their _____ I will write it.
Exodus 24:12 The stone _____ with the _____ and the commandment which I have written for their _____ *Unscramble the word to find the answer* The Old Covenant shows us our ___ ___ ___ (ins)	**Jeremiah 31:34** I will _____ their _____ and their _____ I will remember no more. *Unscramble the word to find the answer* The New Covenant forgives our ___ ___ ___ (ins)

All right! Don't forget to practice your memory verse!

THE OFFERING OF JESUS CHRIST

"We're here!" Molly announced as they hopped out of the Jeep at the House of Caiaphas. "Is this where Peter denied Jesus the night Jesus was arrested?"

"Yes it is. Look over there. That's a statue depicting Peter's denials." Uncle Jake pointed into a courtyard where a statue with Peter, a Roman guard, two women, and a column with a rooster on top stood. "Let's go inside the church. We can go down to the dungeon and then into the pit. The pit is where some people believe Jesus spent His last terrible night being cruelly beaten before He went to the cross. Can you imagine what that last night was like for Jesus?"

Let's talk to God and then look at WHY Jesus offered Himself for us.

We looked at part of Hebrews 10 in Week 5, but today we need to get the details. So turn to page 217 and read Hebrews 10:1-10. Mark these key words:

God (draw a purple triangle and color it yellow)

Jesus (draw a purple cross and color it yellow)

sin (color it brown)

blood (draw three dots of blood)

offering (offer, offered, offerings) (circle it in red)

Don't forget to mark your pronouns! And mark anything that tells you WHEN by drawing a green clock or green circle like this . Ask the 5 W's and an H questions.

Hebrews 10:1 WHAT do we see about the Law (the Old Covenant)?

It was only a _____ of the good things to come.
It can never make _____ those who draw near.

Hebrews 10:3 WHAT were those sacrifices for?

A _____ of _____ year by year

Hebrews 10:4 WHAT do we see about the blood of the sacrificed bulls and goats?

"It is _____ for the blood of bulls and goats

to take away sin."

Hebrews 10:7 WHY did Jesus come?

To do God's _____

Hebrews 10:8 WHAT did God not desire or take pleasure in?

"_____ and offerings and whole burnt offerings"

for sin

Hebrews 10:9 WHAT is taken away?

The f__ __ __ __

The writer of Hebrews is talking about the first covenant. Do you remember what the first covenant was? WHAT is the name of the covenant God gave Moses?

The _____ of _____

Hebrews 10:9 WHAT is established?

The _____

WHAT is this covenant?

The _____ covenant

Hebrews 10:10 HOW are we sanctified?

"Through the _____ of the _____ of

_____ _____ _____ for all."

God took away the Covenant of Law (the first covenant) because it was only a shadow of better things to come (the New Covenant)! The Covenant of Law could not take away sin. It could only remind people of their sin. God established the New Covenant so that we could be sanctified.

Sanctified means "to be set apart, to be made holy." There is *only one way* we are set apart for God, and that's through the offering of Jesus Christ's body: "[God] made Him who knew no sin to be sin on our behalf, so that we might become the righteousness of God in Him" (2 Corinthians 5:21).

Isn't it amazing that God, in His mercy, provided His Son to save us? Wow!

All right, treasure hunter, where are we headed next? Pull out your treasure map of Jerusalem (page 94), and locate "H-7." Fill in the blanks to write out our next location.

V__ __ D__ __ __ __ __ __ __

Don't forget to practice your memory verse!

DAY FIVE

FORGIVEN FOREVER

"This is a cool road, Uncle Jake," Molly said as they walked down the Via Dolorosa. "Does *Via Dolorosa* mean 'the Way of Sorrows'?"

"Yes. Many people believe that this is the road Jesus carried the cross on the way to the crucifixion."

"Jesus went through a lot for us," Max said.

"He sure did, Max," Uncle Jake agreed. "As we walk down the road, let's think about what Jesus did for us so that our sins could be forgiven and remembered no more."

Okay, treasure hunter, ask God for His help. Then turn to page 218. Read Hebrews 10:11-23 and mark these key words:

God (draw a purple triangle and color it yellow)

Jesus (draw a purple cross and color it yellow)

Holy Spirit (draw a purple ⌒ and color it yellow)

covenant (oath) (draw a yellow box around it and color it red)

sin (sins, lawless deeds, these things) (color it brown)

blood (draw three dots of blood)

offering (offer, offered, offerings) (circle it in red)

heart (draw a red heart)

veil (box it in purple and put a red tear down the middle)

Don't forget to mark the pronouns. And mark anything that tells you WHEN by drawing a green clock 🕐 or green circle like this ○ .

Find out what Jesus did for us by asking the 5 W's and an H questions.

Hebrews 10:11 WHAT can never take away sins?

The same _____ offered time after time.

Hebrews 10:12 WHAT did Jesus offer?

_____

Hebrews 10:14 WHAT did Jesus' offering do?

_____

Hebrews 10:16 WHAT covenant is this?

_____

Hebrews 10:16 WHERE will God put His laws?

_____

Hebrews 10:17 WHAT do we discover about our sins?

_____

Hebrews 10:18 WHY is there no longer any offering for sin?

Because there is f__ __ __ __ __ __ __ __ __ __ of sins

Hebrews 10:19 HOW can we have confidence to enter the holy place?

_____

Hebrews 10:19-20 WHAT is the new and living way Jesus inaugurated (started) for us?

We enter the holy place by the _____ of Jesus,

through the _____, that is, His _____.

Remember, the veil formed a barrier in the Jewish temple between the holy place and the holy of holies. And the holy of holies represented God's presence with His people. But only the high priest could go into the holies of holies, and then only one time a year to make an offering for sin. When Jesus died for our sins, the veil was torn so we could come into the presence of God. To enter into the New Covenant, we have to come through the veil (the flesh of Jesus). Jesus is the *only* way to God!

Hebrews 10:21 WHAT do we have?

_____

Hebrews 10:22 WHAT happens to our evil conscience and our bodies when we put our faith in Jesus?

_____

Isn't that fantastic! Jesus becomes our High Priest. We can enter into God's presence because we have been forgiven and washed clean!

Have you ever felt guilty because you sinned? If you have, write out what you did that made you feel that way.

_____

_____

Because of the torn veil, you can come directly into God's presence.

So HOW are you forgiven? WHAT do you have to do? Pull out God's Map and look up and read 1 John 1:9.

1 John 1:9 WHAT do you have to do to have your sins forgiven?

_____

1 John 1:9 Then WHAT will God do?

_____

_____

Awesome! When we confess our sins, God forgives us and cleanses us of *all* unrighteousness. Remember, Jesus offered *one* sacrifice for all time. And then He sat down at the right hand of God. There is *only* one way to be forgiven and have your sins washed away—through *believing in Jesus Christ, confessing your sins, and turning your life over to Him.* When you enter into the

New Covenant through Jesus, God will put His laws on your heart and wash you clean.

Way to go! Say your memory verse out loud to a grown-up to remind you of this New Covenant God writes on your heart!

How are we able to obey God when we enter into the New Covenant? WHAT will help us? You'll find out next week.

THE POWER OF THE NEW COVENANT

an you believe this is our last week in Israel? Look at all we have discovered about God's covenants of salvation. We saw how God promised the "seed"—Jesus Christ— would come through both the Abrahamic and Davidic covenants. We also saw how the sons of Israel broke the Old Covenant and how God, in His love and mercy, provided the New Covenant through Jesus Christ to forgive our sins.

Grab your map and flashlights. This is going to be a great week as we dig for treasure to find out what makes the New Covenant soooooo powerful.

DAY ONE

THE PROMISE

"Hey, guys, guess what?" Uncle Jake asked and then grinned. "I have a special adventure for you. I've arranged for us to participate in an archeological dig."

"All right!" Max said as he and Molly high-fived. "I was hoping we'd get to go on a dig while we were here."

Sam caught their excitement and ran around in circles, barking and wagging his tail. Max laughed and put Sam in the Jeep so they could head for the dig site.

Okay, treasure hunter, grab your Jerusalem treasure map (on page 94). Look at "I-3." That's the site of our archeological dig this week.

"We're here!" Uncle Jake announced. "Grab your gear and talk to God so we can start digging for God's treasure."

Okay, treasure hunter, keep your eyes open as you dig for the next clue in our hunt for the treasure.

"I found it!" Molly waved a dirty envelope at Max. She opened it. "It's another code. It looks like the alphabet code. We need to write the letter that comes *before* the letter that is written in the regular alphabet. Let's crack the code."

Alphabet Code

A B C D E F G H I J K L M N O P Q R S T U V W X Y Z

Secret Message

QPXFS

Max looked at Uncle Jake, "We've cracked the code, but what does it mean?"

"Well..." Uncle Jake paused. "When we enter into the New Covenant with God, He gives us the power to do the things He wants us to do. But where does that power come from? We know it's not from ourselves because man couldn't keep the Old Covenant. That's why God had to give us a New Covenant. So we need to find out where we get the power to please God. Let's pull out God's Map, and then ask for His help."

In God's Map, look up and read John 7:37-39.

John 7:39 WHO is Jesus speaking of? WHO will those who believe receive?

_____

WHEN would the Spirit be given?

After J__ __ __ __ was _____.

Read Acts 1:4-8 (printed after the key word list) and mark these key words:

Spirit (draw a purple mountain and color it yellow)

promise (put a blue "P" over it)

power (draw a red stick of dynamite)

Mark anything that tells you WHEN by drawing a green clock or green circle like this ◯ .

Acts 1:4-8

4 Gathering them together, He commanded them not to leave Jerusalem, but to wait for what the Father had promised, "Which," He said, "you heard of from Me;

5 for John baptized with water, but you will be baptized with the Holy Spirit not many days from now."

6 So when they had come together, they were asking Him, saying, "Lord, is it at this time You are restoring the kingdom to Israel?"

7 He said to them, "It is not for you to know times or epochs which the Father has fixed by His own authority;

8 but you will receive power when the Holy Spirit has come upon you; and you shall be My witnesses both in Jerusalem, and in all Judea and Samaria, and even to the remotest part of the earth."

Now dig for treasure by asking the 5 W's and an H questions.

Acts 1:4 WHAT were they to wait for?

_____

Acts 1:5 WHAT would happen "not many days from now"?

_____

Acts 1:8 WHAT will they receive when the Holy Spirit comes on them?

P__ __ __ __!

All right! You have just dug up a very important treasure! You have discovered you receive power when you receive the Holy Spirit. WHEN do you receive the Holy Spirit? We'll find out soon!

At archeological digs, workers sift through buckets of soil to find all the artifacts, even the tiny ones. Let's sift some soil to discover this week's memory verse.

Look at the sifting screen on the next page. You will sift through all of the words to find the memory verse:

- Cross out all the words that are part of the earth: sand, clay, mud, and silt.

- Next, cross out all the rocks: sandstone, shale, slate, granite, and marble.

- Sift out all the minerals by crossing out graphite, flint, mica, and gypsum.

- Now sift out the crystals by crossing out quartz and salt.

Good job! Now, starting at the top of your screen, write the words that remain from left to right on the blanks below the puzzle.

But	granite	slate	you	marble
quartz	will	sand	mica	receive
silt	power	salt	when	mud
mica	gypsum	the	flint	Holy
Spirit	sandstone	slate	has	shale
gypsum	come	granite	sand	upon
you	salt	silt	Acts	clay
quartz	1	mud	8	marble

___ ___ ___ ___ ___

___ ___ ___ ___ ___ ___

___ ___ ___ ___

___ __ : ___

Way to go! Practice saying this verse, three times in a row, three times today.

DAY TWO

SEALED WITH THE HOLY SPIRIT

"Come quick, Uncle Jake! I found something. Look!" Max cried out as he brushed away the dirt around an object lodged in the ground.

"You're right, Max! Be careful. You're doing a great job scraping away the dirt from your find."

How about you, treasure hunter? Are you ready for a big find? Talk to God, and then get ready to scrape away the dirt to find out WHEN we receive the Holy Spirit.

Pull out God's Map. Look up and read Acts 2:38-39.

Acts 2:38 WHEN do you receive the gift of the Holy Spirit?

You receive the Holy Spirit when you r__ __ __ __ __

and receive f__ __ __ __ __ __ __ __ __ __ of your

s__ __ __ and are b__ __ __ __ __ __ __ in the name of

J__ __ __ __   C__ __ __ __ __.

Read Ephesians 1:13-14 (printed after the key words) and mark these key words.

Holy Spirit (draw a purple ⌒ and color it yellow)

Him (this references Jesus in these verses) (draw a purple cross and color it yellow)

Ephesians 1:13-14

13 In Him, you also, after listening to the message of truth, the gospel of your salvation—having also believed, you were sealed in Him with the Holy Spirit of promise,

14 who is given as a pledge of our inheritance, with a view to the redemption of God's own possession, to the praise of His glory.

Ephesians 1:13 WHAT do you have to do to be sealed with the Holy Spirit?

1. L__ __ __ __ __ to the _____ of _____, the

   _____ of your _____

2. B__ __ __ __ __ __ the gospel

Ephesians 1:13-14 WHAT do you learn about the Holy Spirit?

He is called the "Holy Spirit of p__ __ __ __ __ __."

The Holy Spirit is g__ __ __ __ as a _____ of our

_____.

The Holy Spirit is our guarantee that God will redeem our bodies when we die! Believers will live forever and ever. We have eternal life!

In God's Map, look up and read Romans 8:9 and 14-17.

Romans 8:9 WHAT do we have to have to belong to God?

_____

Romans 8:14 WHO are the sons of God?

_____

_____

Romans 8:16 WHAT does the Spirit testify to our spirit?

_____

Wow! We receive the Holy Spirit when we listen to the gospel, repent (change our mind about sin), and believe in the gospel—the Good News that Jesus died for our sins and paid for them once and for all and rose from the dead. When we believe the gospel, the Holy Spirit comes to live inside us.

The Holy Spirit is given as a promise of our inheritance. He is the guarantee we are going to heaven and that we have eternal life. Romans 8 tells us that if we don't have the Holy Spirit in us, then we are *not* children of God. It is God's Spirit in us that gives us the power to walk in God's ways. Without His power inside us, we just can't do it. *Amazing!*

Don't forget to practice your memory verse!

Living by Faith or the Law?

"Wow, Max. That is so great!" Molly said as she looked at Max's find. " I can't believe you found a real artifact."

"Me neither. This is a cool coin. Too bad I can't keep it. But I know people can't keep what they find on a dig. Artifacts have to go to museums to be studied. Hey, look at Sam's nose! It's dirty from where he's been digging in the dirt pit."

Uncle Jake laughed. "It was nice of Dr. Camden to make a special place just for Sam since he can't help us in the real dig area. Keep your eyes open! There might be a clue in all this dirt."

"I bet I find it first!" Molly called out as she climbed back into the pit.

"We'll just see about that," Max countered.

Okay, treasure hunter, keep your eyes open as you dig for the next clue in our hunt for treasure. We need to find out how we are to live now that we are in the New Covenant. Do we live by faith or do we have to still follow the law? Talk to God, and then we'll find out.

Turn to page 215. Read Galatians 3 and mark these key words:

law (draw black tablets)

faith (believe) (draw a purple book and color it green)

Spirit (draw a purple ⌒ and color it yellow)

promise (put a blue "P" over it)

covenant (draw a yellow box around it and color it red)

Hunt for the treasure by asking those 5 W's and an H questions.

Galatians 3:2 HOW did we receive the Spirit?

By h__ __ __ __ __ __ with f__ __ __ __

Galatians 3:6 HOW was Abraham made righteous (made right with God)?

He _____ God.

Galatians 3:8 HOW would God justify the Gentiles?

By _____

Galatians 3:8 WHAT did God preach to Abraham?

The _____

The gospel is the Good News that Jesus Christ, the Son of God, came into the world to die on the cross to save sinners like you and me. Jesus died and was buried, but He rose again on the third day—never to die again. Isn't that *awesome!*

Galatians 3:9 WHO are blessed with Abraham, the believer?

"Those who are of _____."

Galatians 3:10 WHO are under a curse?

Those who "are of the w__ __ __ __ of the _____."

Galatians 3:10 WHY does this curse matter to us?

We are cursed *if* we are under the works of the law but don't "_____ by all things written in the book of the _____, to _____ them."

Galatians 3:11 HOW are we justified, made righteous?

By _____

Galatians 3:13 WHAT did Christ redeem us from?

The _____ of the _____

Galatians 3:14 WHAT promise will we receive through faith?

The promise of the _____

Galatians 3:17 WHAT can't the law do?

Invalidate a _____ ratified by God or nullify

the _____

Galatians 3:18 WHAT is our inheritance based on?

God granted it to Abraham by means of a _____.

Galatians 3:19 WHY did God give the law?

Because of _____

Galatians 3:19 HOW long was the law for?

Until the _____ would come

WHO is the "seed"? _____

Galatians 3:22 WHAT do we see about the Scripture?

It _____ up everyone under _____

Galatians 3:22 HOW is the promise given?

By _____ in _____ _____

Galatians 3:22 WHO is it given to?

To those who _____

Galatians 3:23 HOW were we kept until faith came?

We were in _____ under the _____.

Custody means "to be under care or protection." Obedience to the law protected people from sinning.

Galatians 3:24 WHAT is the law?

It is "our _____ to lead us to _____, so that we may be _____ by _____."

Galatians 3:25 WHY don't we need a tutor (a teacher or instructor) anymore?

_____ has come.

Galatians 3:26 WHAT are we if we have faith in Jesus Christ?

_____ of _____

Galatians 3:27 WHAT have we done if we are baptized into Christ?

We have _____ ourselves with _____.

Galatians 3:29 WHO are we if we belong to Christ?

"_____ descendants, _____ according to

_____"

Are you ready for another puzzle, treasure hunter? Find all the words you put in the blanks for Day 3 in the following Word Search. Remember, if a word is used more than once in the Day 3 blanks, you only need to find and circle it one time in the puzzle.

S	N	O	i	S	S	E	R	G	S	N	A	R	T
D	E	i	F	i	T	S	U	j	F	C	B	E	i
D	E	V	E	i	L	E	B	C	L	Y	R	S	R
C	O	V	E	N	A	N	T	O	Y	O	A	i	i
B	E	L	i	E	V	E	T	D	O	G	H	M	P
T	S	i	R	H	C	H	T	i	A	F	A	O	S
S	R	i	E	H	E	A	R	i	N	G	M	R	U
N	i	S	Y	D	O	T	S	U	C	R	S	P	S
M	R	O	F	R	E	P	L	E	P	S	O	G	E
A	B	i	D	E	S	R	U	C	N	E	W	N	j
R	O	T	U	T	S	K	R	O	W	E	A	Z	L
S	H	U	T	T	q	X	S	N	D	D	L	V	q

All right! Did you see that the two reasons God gave people the Law was to show them their sins and to keep them from sinning? The law was to lead people to Jesus Christ so they could be made right with God.

The Law couldn't save people, but Jesus did! Isn't that great? God sent Jesus Christ to save us from our sin. We no longer live under the law, but we live by the Holy Spirit because Jesus Christ set us free from sin's power. The Law (the Old Covenant) is taken away. It is replaced by the New Covenant. The Old Covenant only showed people their sins. It couldn't give people the power to overcome sin. But the New Covenant does! What a treasure!

Practice your memory verse to remind you that if you are a child of God, His Spirit lives inside you!

Way to go!

DAY FOUR

ADOPTED BY GOD

"Did you enjoy the dig?" Uncle Jake asked as they cleaned up after their excavation.

"We sure did!" Max and Molly exclaimed while Sam jumped up to give Uncle Jake a good face-licking.

"Get down, Sam!" Max ordered. "Come here and let me wipe your dirty paws. "Hey! What's on Sam's paw? I can't believe it, Uncle Jake. You put a code on Sam's paw! Get out the Jerusalem treasure map, Molly. Sam has the clue to where we're going next."

Okay, treasure hunter, look at the Jerusalem map (page 94). Our next location is "J-3." Write the name of where we're going on the line.

_____

"Wow!" Molly said as they walked to the Gihon Springs. This is fantastic. Are we going to go all the way through Hezekiah's Tunnel to the pool of Siloam?"

"We sure are!" Uncle Jake answered. "But before we go inside, we need to find out WHO we are in the New Covenant. Let's talk to God and get started."

Read Galatians 4:4-7 (printed after the key word) and mark this key word:

 Spirit (draw a purple ⌒⌒ and color it yellow)

Galatians 4:4-7

4 But when the fullness of the time came, God sent forth His Son, born of a woman, born under the Law,

5 so that He might redeem those who were under the Law, that we might receive the adoption as sons.

6 Because you are sons, God has sent forth the Spirit of His Son into our hearts, crying, "Abba! Father!"

7 Therefore you are no longer a slave, but a son; and if a son, then an heir through God.

Galatians 4:4 WHAT did God do in the fullness of time?

_____

Galatians 4:5 WHY did Jesus come?

To "_____ those who were under the _____, that we might receive the _____ as _____"

Galatians 4:6 WHAT did God put in our hearts?

_____

Galatians 4:6 WHY did God do this?

Because we are _____

Galatians 4:7 WHAT are we no longer?

_____

Galatians 4:7 WHAT are we?

A _____ and _____ through God

Isn't that wonderful? God sent Jesus to set us free! We are no longer slaves. We are sons and daughters of God! God gives us the Spirit of His Son to live in us. God has given us an inheritance.

Great work! HOW are we to live now that we have been set free? We'll find out tomorrow. Don't forget to practice your verse.

LiViNG THE NEW COVENANT LiFe

"This is so cool!" Max said as they made their way inside the tunnel. "I can't believe we are walking *under* the City of David in Hezekiah's tunnels."

"Look at those marks on the wall," Molly said.

"That's the 'Siloam inscription,' an ancient text found in the tunnels," Uncle Jake explained. "Keep going! Just a little further."

While Uncle Jake, Max, Molly, and Sam make their way through the tunnels, let's talk to God and then discover how we are to live a "New Covenant life."

Turn to page 222. Read Galatians 5:16-25 and mark these key words:

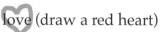 love (draw a red heart)

flesh (draw a brown arrow pointing down)

Spirit (draw a purple ⌒ and color it yellow)

Find the treasure by asking the 5 W's and an H questions.

Galatians 5:16 HOW do we keep from "giving in" to our flesh?

_____

Galatians 5:17 WHAT is the flesh in opposition to?

_____

Galatians 5:18 HOW are we *not* under the law?

_____

Galatians 5:19-21 WHAT are the deeds of the flesh?

_____

_____

_____

_____

Galatians 5:21 WHAT happens if we practice the deeds of the flesh?

_____

Galatians 5:22-23 WHAT is the fruit of the Spirit?

"_____, _____, _____, _____,

_____, _____, _____,

_____, _____-_____"

Galatians 5:24 WHAT do you do if you belong to Christ?

_____

Galatians 5:25-26 WHAT else are you to do?

L__ __ __ by the _____ and w__ __ __ by the

_____. Let us not become _____

_____

When we enter into the New Covenant, God puts His Spirit in us and we are changed. But we are still made of flesh that wants to sin. God tells us *we must walk by the Spirit* so we won't "give in" to our flesh. We are to crucify (put to death) our flesh. That means we are to say *no* to what we want when it is something God doesn't want.

Think about the "deeds of the flesh" Paul listed in his letter to the Galatians. Do you keep yourself pure? Being pure means you say *no* when something you want goes against God. Do you do things you shouldn't be doing? How do you dress? If you are a girl, do you dress to look older than you are? Are your clothes too tight or too short? If you are a guy, are your pants so baggy they hang too low on your body?

Write out how you are keeping yourself pure.

_____

_____

_____

Do you have any idols in your life? Idols are anything you put *before* or *in front* of God, such as playing a sport, texting, or watching TV. WHAT do you put before God?

_____

_____

Do you argue or get along with others? Do you lose your temper? Do you stir up trouble? If you do any of these things, write them down.

_____

_____

Are you jealous of someone? Do you envy what others have or how they look? Explain how you are jealous or envious of others.

_____

_____

These are all "deeds of the flesh." God tells us that anyone who practices these things as habits *will not* inherit the kingdom of heaven. Now, this doesn't mean you won't ever get angry, jealous, or make a mistake. You may mess up (sin), but God will forgive you *if you confess your sin and turn away from it.* If the Spirit is living in you, you can't keep doing it!

Think about the fruit of the Spirit. Do you love others? Do you put others first or do you have to have your way? Do you have to have the best for yourself? Explain.

_____

_____

Do you reach out to kids who may not have friends or who feel left out? Do you invite them to come to your house or go places with you?

_____

Do you have joy? Think about this by spelling joy like this:

J is for Jesus.
O is for others.
Y is for yourself.

If you remember Jesus first, then others, and then yourself last, you will have joy!

Do you have peace? Do you believe God will do what He says? That He will take care of you? _____ Yes _____ No

Are you patient with others? Or do you throw up your hands, roll your eyes, and murmur under your breath at your parents or others? Write out how you are patient with people.

_____

_____

Are you kind? Or do you laugh and make fun of others because of the way they look or the things they do? Share how you are kind.

_____

_____

Do others see goodness and faithfulness in you? Would someone describe you as good? _____ Yes _____ No

Can you be trusted? _____ Yes _____ No

Are you gentle? Share how you are considerate of others.

_____

_____

_____

Are you proud or humble? _____

Do you have self-control or do you get mad and lose your temper?

_____

Write out the characteristics of the Spirit you see in yourself.

_____

_____

_____

These characteristics show whether the Holy Spirit is living in you. Remember, in the New Covenant you have the power to do what God says is right because you have the Holy Spirit living in you! If there is no power, then you aren't saved.

Find a grown-up and say your memory verse out loud. Ask that person when they became a child of God.

GOD'S PRICELESS TREASURE

"Just a little further, kids!" Uncle Jake encouraged.

"Hey, Uncle Jake, what is that?" Max asked as he stared at a small chest inside the tunnel.

Molly stared at it too.

"Ah..." Uncle Jake smiled. "Why don't you open it and find out?"

Max and Molly walked up to the chest. Molly aimed her flashlight at the chest while Sam sniffed at it. Max lifted the lid. Inside was this message:

All right! Way to go! You have taken an incredible journey through the land of Israel to crack the covenant code. Just look at all you discovered as you hunted down God's priceless treasure!

You know *covenant* is a solemn, binding agreement, a compact that is made by passing through pieces of flesh. It is a lifelong promise that is never to be broken. God is faithful to covenant! He is a covenant-keeping God.

You discovered that man couldn't keep the Old Covenant. God gave that covenant to show people how to live until the New Covenant would come and replace it. The Old Covenant showed people their sin, but the New Covenant takes away our sins and gives us the power to overcome sin. God loves us so much that He gave His only begotten Son to save everyone who chooses to believe in Jesus Christ.

You also learned that when you enter into the New Covenant with Jesus, you get to put on His robe of righteousness. You get to "put on Jesus," and He put on your robe by leaving heaven to become a man and die for your sins.

And you discovered Satan is your enemy, but you don't have to worry because when you enter into covenant with Jesus, your enemies become His enemies. Put your armor on and know that Jesus has your back!

In your quest to crack the covenant code, you saw there is a cost to entering into covenant with Jesus. Jesus gave Himself up for you, and you have to give up yourself for Him. You need to give Jesus Christ everything. When you do, He becomes your Covenant Partner and saves you from sin. He gives you His strength, He loves and protects you, He takes on your enemies, He is with you always, He gives you eternal life, and He gives you the gift of His Holy Spirit so you can have the *power* you need to live your life in Him. *Whew!* Isn't that *awesome*?

You have done an amazing job! Never forget that if you have entered into the New Covenant, you are connected with your Covenant Partner forever.

We are so proud of you! You have done a lot of hard work. And now you know the truth. You have discovered the treasure! Will you take what you learned and use it by becoming Jesus' partner in the New Covenant? We hope so!

See you soon for another adventure in God's Word. Shalom!

Molly, Max, and

(Sam)

PUZZLE ANSWERS

Page 17

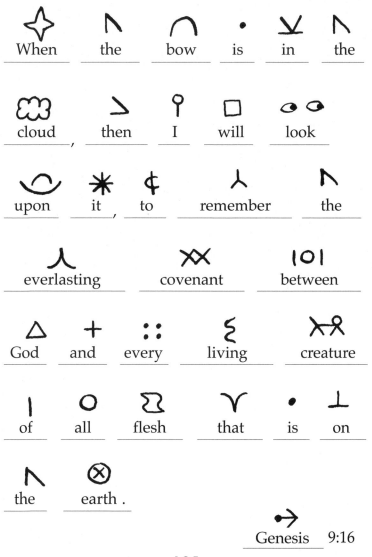

When the bow is in the

cloud, then I will look

upon it, to remember the

everlasting covenant between

God and every living creature

of all flesh that is on

the earth.

Genesis 9:16

Page 51

"<u>For</u> <u>God</u> so <u>loved</u> the <u>world</u>, that <u>He</u> <u>gave</u> His <u>only</u> <u>begotten</u> <u>Son</u>, that <u>whoever</u> <u>believes</u> in <u>Him</u> shall not <u>perish</u>, but have <u>eternal</u> <u>life</u>." John 3:<u>16</u>

Page 58

Page 70

"Put on the full armor of God, so that you will be able to stand firm against the schemes of the devil." Ephesians 6:11

Page 99

"And <u>Mizpah</u>, for <u>he</u> <u>said</u>, "<u>May</u> the LORD <u>watch</u> <u>between</u> <u>you</u> and <u>me</u> when we are <u>absent</u> <u>one</u> from the <u>other</u>." <u>Genesis</u> 31:49

Page 103

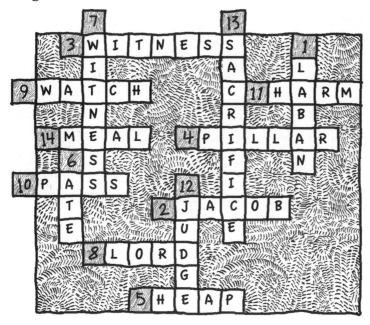

Page 125

"Whoever does not carry his own cross and come after Me cannot be My disciple." Luke 14:27

Page 141

"Then he took the book of the covenant and read it in the hearing of the people; and they said, 'All that the LORD has spoken we will do, and we will be obedient!' " Exodus 24:7

Page 158

"But this is the <u>covenant</u> which I will make with the <u>house</u> of <u>Israel</u> after those days," declares the LORD, "I will put My <u>law</u> within them and on their <u>heart</u> I will <u>write</u> it; and I will be their <u>God</u> and they shall be My <u>people</u>." <u>Jeremiah</u> 31:33

Page 175

But	~~granite~~	~~slate~~	you	~~marble~~
~~quartz~~	will	~~sand~~	~~mica~~	receive
~~silt~~	power	~~salt~~	when	~~mud~~
~~mica~~	~~gypsum~~	the	~~flint~~	Holy
Spirit	~~sandstone~~	~~slate~~	has	~~shale~~
~~gypsum~~	come	~~granite~~	~~sand~~	upon
you	~~salt~~	~~silt~~	Acts	~~clay~~
~~quartz~~	1	~~mud~~	8	~~marble~~

"But you will receive power when the Holy Spirit has come upon you." Acts 1:8

Page 183

OBSERVATION WORKSHEETS

GENESIS 6:5-22

5   Then the LORD saw that the wickedness of man was great on the earth, and that every intent of the thoughts of his heart was only evil continually.

6   The LORD was sorry that He had made man on the earth, and He was grieved in His heart.

7   The LORD said, "I will blot out man whom I have created from the face of the land, from man to animals to creeping things and to birds of the sky; for I am sorry that I have made them."

8   But Noah found favor in the eyes of the LORD.

9   These are the records of the generations of Noah. Noah was a righteous man, blameless in his time; Noah walked with God.

10   Noah became the father of three sons: Shem, Ham, and Japheth.

11   Now the earth was corrupt in the sight of God, and the earth was filled with violence.

12   God looked on the earth, and behold, it was corrupt; for all flesh had corrupted their way upon the earth.

13   Then God said to Noah, "The end of all flesh has come before Me; for the earth is filled with violence because of them; and behold, I am about to destroy them with the earth.

14   "Make for yourself an ark of gopher wood; you shall make the ark with rooms, and shall cover it inside and out with pitch.

15   "This is how you shall make it: the length of the ark three hundred cubits, its breadth fifty cubits, and its height thirty cubits.

16   "You shall make a window for the ark, and finish it to a cubit from the top; and set the door of the ark in the side of it; you shall make it with lower, second, and third decks.

17   "Behold, I, even I am bringing the flood of water upon the earth, to destroy all flesh in which is the breath of life, from under heaven; everything that is on the earth shall perish.

18   "But I will establish My covenant with you; and you shall enter the ark—you and your sons and your wife, and your sons' wives with you.

19 "And of every living thing of all flesh, you shall bring two of every kind into the ark, to keep them alive with you; they shall be male and female.

20 "Of the birds after their kind, and of the animals after their kind, of every creeping thing of the ground after its kind, two of every kind will come to you to keep them alive.

21 "As for you, take for yourself some of all food which is edible, and gather it to yourself; and it shall be for food for you and for them."

22 Thus Noah did; according to all that God had commanded him, so he did.

GENESiS 9:8-19

8 Then God spoke to Noah and to his sons with him, saying,

9 "Now behold, I Myself do establish My covenant with you, and with your descendants after you;

10 and with every living creature that is with you, the birds, the cattle, and every beast of the earth with you; of all that comes out of the ark, even every beast of the earth.

11 "I establish My covenant with you; and all flesh shall never again be cut off by the water of the flood, neither shall there again be a flood to destroy the earth."

12 God said, "This is the sign of the covenant which I am making between Me and you and every living creature that is with you, for all successive generations;

13 I set My bow in the cloud, and it shall be for a sign of a covenant between Me and the earth.

14 "It shall come about, when I bring a cloud over the earth, that the bow will be seen in the cloud,

15 and I will remember My covenant, which is between Me and you and every living creature of all flesh; and never again shall the water become a flood to destroy all flesh.

16 "When the bow is in the cloud, then I will look upon it, to remember the everlasting covenant between God and every living creature of all flesh that is on the earth."

17 And God said to Noah, "This is the sign of the covenant which I have established between Me and all flesh that is on the earth."

18 Now the sons of Noah who came out of the ark were Shem and Ham and Japheth; and Ham was the father of Canaan.

19 These three were the sons of Noah, and from these the whole earth was populated.

GENESIS 15

1 After these things the word of the LORD came to Abram in a vision, saying,

> "Do not fear, Abram,
>
> I am a shield to you;
>
> Your reward shall be very great."

2 Abram said, "O Lord GOD, what will You give me, since I am childless, and the heir of my house is Eliezer of Damascus?"

3 And Abram said, "Since You have given no offspring to me, one born in my house is my heir."

4 Then behold, the word of the LORD came to him, saying, "This man will not be your heir; but one who will come forth from your own body, he shall be your heir."

5 And He took him outside and said, "Now look toward the heavens, and count the stars, if you are able to count them." And He said to him, "So shall your descendants be."

6 Then he believed in the LORD; and He reckoned it to him as righteousness.

7 And He said to him, "I am the LORD who brought you out of Ur of the Chaldeans, to give you this land to possess it."

8 He said, "O Lord GOD, how may I know that I will possess it?"

9 So He said to him, "Bring Me a three year old heifer, and a three year old female goat, and a three year old ram, and a turtledove, and a young pigeon."

10 Then he brought all these to Him and cut them in two, and laid each half opposite the other; but he did not cut the birds.

11 The birds of prey came down upon the carcasses, and Abram drove them away.

12 Now when the sun was going down, a deep sleep fell upon Abram; and behold, terror and great darkness fell upon him.

13 God said to Abram, "Know for certain that your descendants will be strangers in a land that is not theirs, where they will be enslaved and oppressed four hundred years.

14 "But I will also judge the nation whom they will serve, and afterward they will come out with many possessions.

15 "As for you, you shall go to your fathers in peace; you will be buried at a good old age.

16 "Then in the fourth generation they will return here, for the iniquity of the Amorite is not yet complete."

17 It came about when the sun had set, that it was very dark, and behold, there appeared a smoking oven and a flaming torch which passed between these pieces.

18 On that day the LORD made a covenant with Abram, saying,

"To your descendants I have given this land,

From the river of Egypt as far as the great river, the river Euphrates:

19 the Kenite and the Kenizzite and the Kadmonite

20 and the Hittite and the Perizzite and the Rephaim

21 and the Amorite and the Canaanite and the Girgashite and the Jebusite."

GENESiS 17:1-24

1 Now when Abram was ninety-nine years old, the LORD appeared to Abram and said to him,

"I am God Almighty;

Walk before Me, and be blameless.

2 "I will establish My covenant between Me and you,

And I will multiply you exceedingly."

3 Abram fell on his face, and God talked with him, saying,

4 "As for Me, behold, My covenant is with you,

And you will be the father of a multitude of nations.

5 "No longer shall your name be called Abram,

But your name shall be Abraham;

For I have made you the father of a multitude of nations.

6 "I will make you exceedingly fruitful, and I will make nations of you, and kings will come forth from you.

7 "I will establish My covenant between Me and you and your descendants after you throughout their generations for an everlasting covenant, to be God to you and to your descendants after you.

8 "I will give to you and to your descendants after you, the land of

your sojournings, all the land of Canaan, for an everlasting possession; and I will be their God."

9 God said further to Abraham, "Now as for you, you shall keep My covenant, you and your descendants after you throughout their generations.

10 "This is My covenant, which you shall keep, between Me and you and your descendants after you: every male among you shall be circumcised.

11 "And you shall be circumcised in the flesh of your foreskin, and it shall be the sign of the covenant between Me and you.

12 "And every male among you who is eight days old shall be circumcised throughout your generations, a servant who is born in the house or who is bought with money from any foreigner, who is not of your descendants.

13 "A servant who is born in your house or who is bought with your money shall surely be circumcised; thus shall My covenant be in your flesh for an everlasting covenant.

14 "But an uncircumcised male who is not circumcised in the flesh of his foreskin, that person shall be cut off from his people; he has broken My covenant."

15 Then God said to Abraham, "As for Sarai your wife, you shall not call her name Sarai, but Sarah shall be her name.

16 "I will bless her, and indeed I will give you a son by her. Then I will bless her, and she shall be a mother of nations; kings of peoples will come from her."

17 Then Abraham fell on his face and laughed, and said in his heart, "Will a child be born to a man one hundred years old? And will Sarah, who is ninety years old, bear a child?"

18 And Abraham said to God, "Oh that Ishmael might live before You!"

19 But God said, "No, but Sarah your wife will bear you a son, and you shall call his name Isaac; and I will establish My covenant with him for an everlasting covenant for his descendants after him.

20 "As for Ishmael, I have heard you; behold, I will bless him, and will make him fruitful and will multiply him exceedingly. He shall become the father of twelve princes, and I will make him a great nation.

21 "But My covenant I will establish with Isaac, whom Sarah will bear to you at this season next year."

22 When He finished talking with him, God went up from Abraham.

23 Then Abraham took Ishmael his son, and all the servants who were born in his house and all who were bought with his money, every male among the men of Abraham's household, and circumcised the flesh of their foreskin in the very same day, as God had said to him.

24 Now Abraham was ninety-nine years old when he was circumcised in the flesh of his foreskin.

EXODUS 6:1-9

1 Then the LORD said to Moses, "Now you shall see what I will do to Pharaoh; for under compulsion he will let them go, and under compulsion he will drive them out of his land."

2 God spoke further to Moses and said to him, "I am the LORD;

3 and I appeared to Abraham, Isaac, and Jacob, as God Almighty, but by My name, LORD, I did not make Myself known to them.

4 "I also established My covenant with them, to give them the land of Canaan, the land in which they sojourned.

5 "Furthermore I have heard the groaning of the sons of Israel, because the Egyptians are holding them in bondage, and I have remembered My covenant.

6 "Say, therefore, to the sons of Israel, ' I am the LORD, and I will bring you out from under the burdens of the Egyptians, and I will deliver you from their bondage. I will also redeem you with an outstretched arm and with great judgments.

7 'Then I will take you for My people, and I will be your God; and you shall know that I am the LORD your God, who brought you out from under the burdens of the Egyptians.

8 'I will bring you to the land which I swore to give to Abraham, Isaac, and Jacob, and I will give it to you for a possession; I am the LORD.' "

9 So Moses spoke thus to the sons of Israel, but they did not listen to Moses on account of their despondency and cruel bondage.

EXODUS 19:1-9

1 In the third month after the sons of Israel had gone out of the land of Egypt, on that very day they came into the wilderness of Sinai.

2 When they set out from Rephidim, they came to the wilderness of Sinai and camped in the wilderness; and there Israel camped in front of the mountain.

3 Moses went up to God, and the LORD called to him from the mountain, saying, "Thus you shall say to the house of Jacob and tell the sons of Israel:

4 'You yourselves have seen what I did to the Egyptians, and how I bore you on eagles' wings, and brought you to Myself.

5 'Now then, if you will indeed obey My voice and keep My covenant, then you shall be My own possession among all the peoples, for all the earth is Mine;

6 and you shall be to Me a kingdom of priests and a holy nation.' These are the words that you shall speak to the sons of Israel."

7 So Moses came and called the elders of the people, and set before them all these words which the LORD had commanded him.

8 All the people answered together and said, "All that the LORD has spoken we will do!" And Moses brought back the words of the people to the LORD.

9 The LORD said to Moses, "Behold, I will come to you in a thick cloud, so that the people may hear when I speak with you and may also believe in you forever." Then Moses told the words of the people to the LORD.

EXODUS 24:3-12

3 Then Moses came and recounted to the people all the words of the LORD and all the ordinances; and all the people answered with one voice and said, "All the words which the LORD has spoken we will do!"

4 Moses wrote down all the words of the LORD. Then he arose early in the morning, and built an altar at the foot of the mountain with twelve pillars for the twelve tribes of Israel.

5 He sent young men of the sons of Israel, and they offered burnt offerings and sacrificed young bulls as peace offerings to the LORD.

6 Moses took half of the blood and put it in basins, and the other half of the blood he sprinkled on the altar.

7 Then he took the book of the covenant and read it in the hearing of the people; and they said, "All that the LORD has spoken we will do, and we will be obedient!"

8 So Moses took the blood and sprinkled it on the people, and said, "Behold the blood of the covenant, which the LORD has made with you in accordance with all these words."

9 Then Moses went up with Aaron, Nadab and Abihu, and seventy of the elders of Israel,

10 and they saw the God of Israel; and under His feet there appeared to be a pavement of sapphire, as clear as the sky itself.

11 Yet He did not stretch out His hand against the nobles of the sons of Israel; and they saw God, and they ate and drank.

12 Now the LORD said to Moses, "Come up to Me on the mountain and remain there, and I will give you the stone tablets with the law and the commandment which I have written for their instruction."

EXODUS 34:27-28

27 Then the LORD said to Moses, "Write down these words, for in accordance with these words I have made a covenant with you and with Israel."

28 So he was there with the LORD forty days and forty nights; he did not eat bread or drink water. And he wrote on the tablets the words of the covenant, the Ten Commandments.

1 SAMUEL 17:55-58

55 Now when Saul saw David going out against the Philistine, he said to Abner the commander of the army, "Abner, whose son is this young man?" And Abner said, "By your life, O king, I do not know."

56 The king said, "You inquire whose son the youth is."

57 So when David returned from killing the Philistine, Abner took him and brought him before Saul with the Philistine's head in his hand.

58 Saul said to him, "Whose son are you, young man?" And David answered, "I am the son of your servant Jesse the Bethlehemite."

1 SAMUEL 18:1-5

1 Now it came about when he had finished speaking to Saul, that the soul of Jonathan was knit to the soul of David, and Jonathan loved him as himself.

2 Saul took him that day and did not let him return to his father's house.

3 Then Jonathan made a covenant with David because he loved him as himself.

4 Jonathan stripped himself of the robe that was on him and gave it to David, with his armor, including his sword and his bow and his belt.

5 So David went out wherever Saul sent him, and prospered; and Saul set him over the men of war. And it was pleasing in the sight of all the people and also in the sight of Saul's servants.

COLOSSIANS 3:1-10

1 Therefore if you have been raised up with Christ, keep seeking the things above, where Christ is, seated at the right hand of God.

2 Set your mind on the things above, not on the things that are on earth.

3 For you have died and your life is hidden with Christ in God.

4 When Christ, who is our life, is revealed, then you also will be revealed with Him in glory.

5 Therefore consider the members of your earthly body as dead to immorality, impurity, passion, evil desire, and greed, which amounts to idolatry.

6 For it is because of these things that the wrath of God will come upon the sons of disobedience,

7 and in them you also once walked, when you were living in them.

8 But now you also, put them all aside: anger, wrath, malice, slander, and abusive speech from your mouth.

9 Do not lie to one another, since you laid aside the old self with its evil practices,

10 and have put on the new self who is being renewed to a true knowledge according to the image of the One who created him.

EPHESIANS 6:10-17

10 Finally, be strong in the Lord and in the strength of His might.

11 Put on the full armor of God, so that you will be able to stand firm against the schemes of the devil.

12 For our struggle is not against flesh and blood, but against the rulers, against the powers, against the world forces of this darkness, against the spiritual forces of wickedness in the heavenly places.

13 Therefore, take up the full armor of God, so that you will be able to resist in the evil day, and having done everything, to stand firm.

14 Stand firm therefore, having girded your loins with truth, and having put on the breastplate of righteousness,

15 and having shod your feet with the preparation of the gospel of peace;

16 in addition to all, taking up the shield of faith with which you will be able to extinguish all the flaming arrows of the evil one.

17 And take the helmet of salvation, and the sword of the Spirit, which is the word of God.

JOHN 15:17-19

17 "This I command you, that you love one another.

18 "If the world hates you, you know that it has hated Me before it hated you.

19 "If you were of the world, the world would love its own; but because you are not of the world, but I chose you out of the world, because of this the world hates you."

JOHN 17:14-17

14 "I have given them Your word; and the world has hated them, because they are not of the world, even as I am not of the world.

15 "I do not ask You to take them out of the world, but to keep them from the evil one.

16 "They are not of the world, even as I am not of the world.

17 "Sanctify them in the truth; Your word is truth."

1 SAMUEL 20

1 Then David fled from Naioth in Ramah, and came and said to Jonathan, "What have I done? What is my iniquity? And what is my sin before your father, that he is seeking my life?"

2 He said to him, "Far from it, you shall not die. Behold, my father does nothing either great or small without disclosing it to me. So why should my father hide this thing from me? It is not so!"

3 Yet David vowed again, saying, "Your father knows well that I have found favor in your sight, and he has said, 'Do not let Jonathan know this, or he will be grieved.' But truly as the LORD lives and as your soul lives, there is hardly a step between me and death."

4 Then Jonathan said to David, "Whatever you say, I will do for you."

5 So David said to Jonathan, "Behold, tomorrow is the new moon, and I ought to sit down to eat with the king. But let me go, that I may hide myself in the field until the third evening.

6 "If your father misses me at all, then say, 'David earnestly asked leave of me to run to Bethlehem his city, because it is the yearly sacrifice there for the whole family.'

7 "If he says, 'It is good,' your servant will be safe; but if he is very angry, know that he has decided on evil.

8 "Therefore deal kindly with your servant, for you have brought your servant into a covenant of the LORD with you. But if there is iniquity in me, put me to death yourself; for why then should you bring me to your father?"

9 Jonathan said, "Far be it from you! For if I should indeed learn that evil has been decided by my father to come upon you, then would I not tell you about it?"

10 Then David said to Jonathan, "Who will tell me if your father answers you harshly?"

11 Jonathan said to David, "Come, and let us go out into the field." So both of them went out to the field.

12 Then Jonathan said to David, "The LORD, the God of Israel, be witness! When I have sounded out my father about this time tomorrow, or the third day, behold, if there is good feeling toward David, shall I not then send to you and make it known to you?

13 "If it please my father to do you harm, may the LORD do so to Jonathan and more also, if I do not make it known to you and send

you away, that you may go in safety. And may the LORD be with you as He has been with my father.

14 "If I am still alive, will you not show me the lovingkindness of the LORD, that I may not die?

15 "You shall not cut off your lovingkindness from my house forever, not even when the LORD cuts off every one of the enemies of David from the face of the earth."

16 So Jonathan made a covenant with the house of David, saying, "May the LORD require it at the hands of David's enemies."

17 Jonathan made David vow again because of his love for him, because he loved him as he loved his own life.

18 Then Jonathan said to him, "Tomorrow is the new moon, and you will be missed because your seat will be empty.

19 "When you have stayed for three days, you shall go down quickly and come to the place where you hid yourself on that eventful day, and you shall remain by the stone Ezel.

20 "I will shoot three arrows to the side, as though I shot at a target.

21 "And behold, I will send the lad, saying, 'Go, find the arrows.' If I specifically say to the lad, 'Behold, the arrows are on this side of you, get them,' then come; for there is safety for you and no harm, as the LORD lives.

22 "But if I say to the youth, 'Behold, the arrows are beyond you,' go, for the LORD has sent you away.

23 "As for the agreement of which you and I have spoken, behold, the LORD is between you and me forever."

24 So David hid in the field; and when the new moon came, the king sat down to eat food.

25 The king sat on his seat as usual, the seat by the wall; then Jonathan rose up and Abner sat down by Saul's side, but David's place was empty.

26 Nevertheless Saul did not speak anything that day, for he thought, "It is an accident, he is not clean, surely he is not clean."

27 It came about the next day, the second day of the new moon, that David's place was empty; so Saul said to Jonathan his son, "Why has the son of Jesse not come to the meal, either yesterday or today?"

28 Jonathan then answered Saul, "David earnestly asked leave of me to go to Bethlehem,

29 for he said, 'Please let me go, since our family has a sacrifice in the

city, and my brother has commanded me to attend. And now, if I have found favor in your sight, please let me get away that I may see my brothers.' For this reason he has not come to the king's table."

30 Then Saul's anger burned against Jonathan and he said to him, "You son of a perverse, rebellious woman! Do I not know that you are choosing the son of Jesse to your own shame and to the shame of your mother's nakedness?

31 "For as long as the son of Jesse lives on the earth, neither you nor your kingdom will be established. Therefore now, send and bring him to me, for he must surely die."

32 But Jonathan answered Saul his father and said to him, "Why should he be put to death? What has he done?"

33 Then Saul hurled his spear at him to strike him down; so Jonathan knew that his father had decided to put David to death.

34 Then Jonathan arose from the table in fierce anger, and did not eat food on the second day of the new moon, for he was grieved over David because his father had dishonored him.

35 Now it came about in the morning that Jonathan went out into the field for the appointment with David, and a little lad was with him.

36 He said to his lad, "Run, find now the arrows which I am about to shoot." As the lad was running, he shot an arrow past him.

37 When the lad reached the place of the arrow which Jonathan had shot, Jonathan called after the lad and said, "Is not the arrow beyond you?"

38 And Jonathan called after the lad, "Hurry, be quick, do not stay!" And Jonathan's lad picked up the arrow and came to his master.

39 But the lad was not aware of anything; only Jonathan and David knew about the matter.

40 Then Jonathan gave his weapons to his lad and said to him, "Go, bring them to the city."

41 When the lad was gone, David rose from the south side and fell on his face to the ground, and bowed three times. And they kissed each other and wept together, but David wept the more.

42 Jonathan said to David, "Go in safety, inasmuch as we have sworn to each other in the name of the LORD, saying, 'The LORD will be between me and you, and between my descendants and your descendants forever.' " Then he rose and departed, while Jonathan went into the city.

GENESIS 31:43-55

43 Then Laban replied to Jacob, "The daughters are my daughters, and the children are my children, and the flocks are my flocks, and all that you see is mine. But what can I do this day to these my daughters or to their children whom they have borne?

44 "So now come, let us make a covenant, you and I, and let it be a witness between you and me."

45 Then Jacob took a stone and set it up as a pillar.

46 Jacob said to his kinsmen, "Gather stones." So they took stones and made a heap, and they ate there by the heap.

47 Now Laban called it Jegar-sahadutha, but Jacob called it Galeed.

48 Laban said, "This heap is a witness between you and me this day." Therefore it was named Galeed,

49 and Mizpah, for he said, "May the LORD watch between you and me when we are absent one from the other.

50 "If you mistreat my daughters, or if you take wives besides my daughters, although no man is with us, see, God is witness between you and me."

51 Laban said to Jacob, "Behold this heap and behold the pillar which I have set between you and me.

52 "This heap is a witness, and the pillar is a witness, that I will not pass by this heap to you for harm, and you will not pass by this heap and this pillar to me, for harm.

53 "The God of Abraham and the God of Nahor, the God of their father, judge between us." So Jacob swore by the fear of his father Isaac.

54 Then Jacob offered a sacrifice on the mountain, and called his kinsmen to the meal; and they ate the meal and spent the night on the mountain.

55 Early in the morning Laban arose, and kissed his sons and his daughters and blessed them. Then Laban departed and returned to his place.

2 SAMUEL 9:1-13

1 Then David said, "Is there yet anyone left of the house of Saul, that I may show him kindness for Jonathan's sake?"

2 Now there was a servant of the house of Saul whose name was

Ziba, and they called him to David; and the king said to him, "Are you Ziba?" And he said, "I am your servant."

3 The king said, "Is there not yet anyone of the house of Saul to whom I may show the kindness of God?" And Ziba said to the king, "There is still a son of Jonathan who is crippled in both feet."

4 So the king said to him, "Where is he?" And Ziba said to the king, "Behold, he is in the house of Machir the son of Ammiel in Lo-debar."

5 Then King David sent and brought him from the house of Machir the son of Ammiel, from Lo-debar.

6 Mephibosheth, the son of Jonathan the son of Saul, came to David and fell on his face and prostrated himself. And David said, "Mephibosheth." And he said, "Here is your servant!"

7 David said to him, "Do not fear, for I will surely show kindness to you for the sake of your father Jonathan, and will restore to you all the land of your grandfather Saul; and you shall eat at my table regularly."

8 Again he prostrated himself and said, "What is your servant, that you should regard a dead dog like me?"

9 Then the king called Saul's servant Ziba and said to him, "All that belonged to Saul and to all his house I have given to your master's grandson.

10 "You and your sons and your servants shall cultivate the land for him, and you shall bring in the produce so that your master's grandson may have food; nevertheless Mephibosheth your master's grandson shall eat at my table regularly." Now Ziba had fifteen sons and twenty servants.

11 Then Ziba said to the king, "According to all that my lord the king commands his servant so your servant will do." So Mephibosheth ate at David's table as one of the king's sons.

12 Mephibosheth had a young son whose name was Mica. And all who lived in the house of Ziba were servants to Mephibosheth.

13 So Mephibosheth lived in Jerusalem, for he ate at the king's table regularly. Now he was lame in both feet.

2 SAMUEL 21:1-14

1 Now there was a famine in the days of David for three years, year after year; and David sought the presence of the LORD. And the

Lord said, "It is for Saul and his bloody house, because he put the Gibeonites to death."

2 So the king called the Gibeonites and spoke to them (now the Gibeonites were not of the sons of Israel but of the remnant of the Amorites, and the sons of Israel made a covenant with them, but Saul had sought to kill them in his zeal for the sons of Israel and Judah).

3 Thus David said to the Gibeonites, "What should I do for you? And how can I make atonement that you may bless the inheritance of the Lord?"

4 Then the Gibeonites said to him, "We have no concern of silver or gold with Saul or his house, nor is it for us to put any man to death in Israel." And he said, "I will do for you whatever you say."

5 So they said to the king, "The man who consumed us and who planned to exterminate us from remaining within any border of Israel,

6 let seven men from his sons be given to us, and we will hang them before the Lord in Gibeah of Saul, the chosen of the Lord." And the king said, "I will give them."

7 But the king spared Mephibosheth, the son of Jonathan the son of Saul, because of the oath of the Lord which was between them, between David and Saul's son Jonathan.

8 So the king took the two sons of Rizpah the daughter of Aiah, Armoni and Mephibosheth whom she had borne to Saul, and the five sons of Merab the daughter of Saul, whom she had borne to Adriel the son of Barzillai the Meholathite.

9 Then he gave them into the hands of the Gibeonites, and they hanged them in the mountain before the Lord, so that the seven of them fell together; and they were put to death in the first days of harvest at the beginning of barley harvest.

10 And Rizpah the daughter of Aiah took sackcloth and spread it for herself on the rock, from the beginning of harvest until it rained on them from the sky; and she allowed neither the birds of the sky to rest on them by day nor the beasts of the field by night.

11 When it was told David what Rizpah the daughter of Aiah, the concubine of Saul, had done,

12 then David went and took the bones of Saul and the bones of Jonathan his son from the men of Jabesh-gilead, who had stolen them from the open square of Beth-shan, where the Philistines had hanged them on the day the Philistines struck down Saul in Gilboa.

13 He brought up the bones of Saul and the bones of Jonathan his son from there, and they gathered the bones of those who had been hanged.

14 They buried the bones of Saul and Jonathan his son in the country of Benjamin in Zela, in the grave of Kish his father; thus they did all that the king commanded, and after that God was moved by prayer for the land.

1 CORiNTHiANS 11:23-32

23 For I received from the Lord that which I also delivered to you, that the Lord Jesus in the night in which He was betrayed took bread;

24 and when He had given thanks, He broke it and said, "This is My body, which is for you; do this in remembrance of Me."

25 In the same way He took the cup also after supper, saying, "This cup is the new covenant in My blood; do this, as often as you drink it, in remembrance of Me."

26 For as often as you eat this bread and drink the cup, you proclaim the Lord's death until He comes.

27 Therefore whoever eats the bread or drinks the cup of the Lord in an unworthy manner, shall be guilty of the body and the blood of the Lord.

28 But a man must examine himself, and in so doing he is to eat of the bread and drink of the cup.

29 For he who eats and drinks, eats and drinks judgment to himself if he does not judge the body rightly.

30 For this reason many among you are weak and sick, and a number sleep.

31 But if we judged ourselves rightly, we would not be judged.

32 But when we are judged, we are disciplined by the Lord so that we will not be condemned along with the world.

GALATiANS 3

1 You foolish Galatians, who has bewitched you, before whose eyes Jesus Christ was publicly portrayed as crucified?

2 This is the only thing I want to find out from you: did you receive the Spirit by the works of the Law, or by hearing with faith?

3 Are you so foolish? Having begun by the Spirit, are you now being perfected by the flesh?

4 Did you suffer so many things in vain—if indeed it was in vain?

5 So then, does He who provides you with the Spirit and works miracles among you, do it by the works of the Law, or by hearing with faith?

6 Even so Abraham believed God, and it was reckoned to him as righteousness.

7 Therefore, be sure that it is those who are of faith who are sons of Abraham.

8 The Scripture, foreseeing that God would justify the Gentiles by faith, preached the gospel beforehand to Abraham, saying, "All the nations will be blessed in you."

9 So then those who are of faith are blessed with Abraham, the believer.

10 For as many as are of the works of the Law are under a curse; for it is written, "Cursed is everyone who does not abide by all things written in the book of the law, to perform them."

11 Now that no one is justified by the Law before God is evident; for, "The righteous man shall live by faith."

12 However, the Law is not of faith; on the contrary, "He who practices them shall live by them."

13 Christ redeemed us from the curse of the Law, having become a curse for us—for it is written, "Cursed is everyone who hangs on a tree"—

14 in order that in Christ Jesus the blessing of Abraham might come to the Gentiles, so that we would receive the promise of the Spirit through faith.

15 Brethren, I speak in terms of human relations: even though it is only a man's covenant, yet when it has been ratified, no one sets it aside or adds conditions to it.

16 Now the promises were spoken to Abraham and to his seed. He does not say, "And to seeds," as referring to many, but rather to one, "And to your seed," that is, Christ.

17 What I am saying is this: the Law, which came four hundred and thirty years later, does not invalidate a covenant previously ratified by God, so as to nullify the promise.

18 For if the inheritance is based on law, it is no longer based on a promise; but God has granted it to Abraham by means of a promise.

19 Why the Law then? It was added because of transgressions, having been ordained through angels by the agency of a mediator, until the seed would come to whom the promise had been made.

20 Now a mediator is not for one party only; whereas God is only one.

21 Is the Law then contrary to the promises of God? May it never be! For if a law had been given which was able to impart life, then righteousness would indeed have been based on law.

22 But the Scripture has shut up everyone under sin, so that the promise by faith in Jesus Christ might be given to those who believe.

23 But before faith came, we were kept in custody under the law, being shut up to the faith which was later to be revealed.

24 Therefore the Law has become our tutor to lead us to Christ, so that we may be justified by faith.

25 But now that faith has come, we are no longer under a tutor.

26 For you are all sons of God through faith in Christ Jesus.

27 For all of you who were baptized into Christ have clothed yourselves with Christ.

28 There is neither Jew nor Greek, there is neither slave nor free man, there is neither male nor female; for you are all one in Christ Jesus.

29 And if you belong to Christ, then you are Abraham's descendants, heirs according to promise.

HEBREWS 10:1-23

1 For the Law, since it has only a shadow of the good things to come and not the very form of things, can never, by the same sacrifices which they offer continually year by year, make perfect those who draw near.

2 Otherwise, would they not have ceased to be offered, because the worshipers, having once been cleansed, would no longer have had consciousness of sins?

3 But in those sacrifices there is a reminder of sins year by year.

4 For it is impossible for the blood of bulls and goats to take away sins.

5 Therefore, when He comes into the world, He says,

"Sacrifice and offering You have not desired,

But a body you have prepared for Me;

6 In whole burnt offerings and sacrifices for sin You have taken no pleasure.

7 "Then I said, 'Behold, I have come (in the scroll of the book it is written of Me) to do Your will, O God.' "

8 After saying above, "Sacrifices and Offerings and whole burnt offerings and sacrifices for sin You have not desired, nor have You taken pleasure in them" (which are offered according to the Law),

9 then He said, "Behold, I have come to do Your will." He takes away the first in order to establish the second.

10 By this will we have been sanctified through the offering of the body of Jesus Christ once for all.

11 Every priest stands daily ministering and offering time after time the same sacrifices, which can never take away sins;

12 but He, having offered one sacrifice for sins for all time, sat down at the right hand of God,

13 waiting from that time onward Until His enemies be made a footstool for His feet.

14 For by one offering He has perfected for all time those who are sanctified.

15 And the Holy Spirit also testifies to us; for after saying,

16 "This is the covenant that I will make with them after those days, says the LORD:

I will put My laws upon their heart,

And on their mind I will write them,"

He then says,

17 "And their sins and their lawless deeds

I will remember no more."

18 Now where there is forgiveness of these things, there is no longer any offering for sin.

19 Therefore, brethren, since we have confidence to enter the holy place by the blood of Jesus,

20 by a new and living way which He inaugurated for us through the veil, that is, His flesh,

21 and since we have a great priest over the house of God,

22 let us draw near with a sincere heart in full assurance of faith,

having our hearts sprinkled clean from an evil conscience and our bodies washed with pure water.

23 Let us hold fast the confession of our hope without wavering, for He who promised is faithful;

LUKE 14:25-33

25 Now large crowds were going along with Him; and He turned and said to them,

26 "If anyone comes to Me, and does not hate his own father and mother and wife and children and brothers and sisters, yes, and even his own life, he cannot be My disciple.

27 "Whoever does not carry his own cross and come after Me cannot be My disciple.

28 "For which one of you, when he wants to build a tower, does not first sit down and calculate the cost to see if he has enough to complete it?

29 "Otherwise, when he has laid a foundation and is not able to finish, all who observe it begin to ridicule him,

30 saying, 'This man began to build and was not able to finish.'

31 "Or what king, when he sets out to meet another king in battle, will not first sit down and consider whether he is strong enough with ten thousand men to encounter the one coming against him with twenty thousand?

32 "Or else, while the other is still far away, he sends a delegation and asks for terms of peace.

33 "So then, none of you can be My disciple who does not give up all his own possessions."

2 SAMUEL 7:1-18

1 Now it came about when the king lived in his house, and the LORD had given him rest on every side from all his enemies,

2 that the king said to Nathan the prophet, "See now, I dwell in a house of cedar, but the ark of God dwells within tent curtains."

3 Nathan said to the king, "Go, do all that is in your mind, for the LORD is with you."

4 But in the same night the word of the LORD came to Nathan, saying,

5 "Go and say to My servant David, 'Thus says the LORD, "Are you the one who should build Me a house to dwell in?

6 "For I have not dwelt in a house since the day I brought up the sons of Israel from Egypt, even to this day; but I have been moving about in a tent, even in a tabernacle.

7 "Wherever I have gone with all the sons of Israel, did I speak a word with one of the tribes of Israel, which I commanded to shepherd My people Israel, saying, 'Why have you not built Me a house of cedar?' "

8 "Now therefore, thus you shall say to My servant David, 'Thus says the LORD of hosts, "I took you from the pasture, from following the sheep, to be ruler over My people Israel.

9 "I have been with you wherever you have gone and have cut off all your enemies from before you; and I will make you a great name, like the names of the great men who are on the earth.

10 "I will also appoint a place for My people Israel and will plant them, that they may live in their own place and not be disturbed again, nor will the wicked afflict them any more as formerly,

11 even from the day that I commanded judges to be over My people Israel; and I will give you rest from all your enemies. The LORD also declares to you that the LORD will make a house for you.

12 "When your days are complete and you lie down with your fathers, I will raise up your descendant after you, who will come forth from you, and I will establish his kingdom.

13 "He shall build a house for My name, and I will establish the throne of his kingdom forever.

14 "I will be a father to him and he will be a son to Me; when he commits iniquity, I will correct him with the rod of men and the strokes of the sons of men,

15 but My lovingkindness shall not depart from him, as I took it away from Saul, whom I removed from before you.

16 "Your house and your kingdom shall endure before Me forever; your throne shall be established forever."' "

17 In accordance with all these words and all this vision, so Nathan spoke to David.

18 Then David the king went in and sat before the LORD, and he said, "Who am I, O Lord GOD, and what is my house, that You have brought me this far?"

JEREMIAH 11:1-11

1 The word which came to Jeremiah from the LORD, saying,

2 "Hear the words of this covenant, and speak to the men of Judah and to the inhabitants of Jerusalem;

3 and say to them, 'Thus says the LORD, the God of Israel, "Cursed is the man who does not heed the words of this covenant

4 which I commanded your forefathers in the day that I brought them out of the land of Egypt, from the iron furnace, saying, 'Listen to My voice, and do according to all which I command you; so you shall be My people, and I will be your God,'

5 in order to confirm the oath which I swore to your forefathers, to give them a land flowing with milk and honey, as it is this day." ' " Then I said, "Amen, O LORD."

6 And the LORD said to me, "Proclaim all these words in the cities of Judah and in the streets of Jerusalem, saying, 'Hear the words of this covenant and do them.

7 'For I solemnly warned your fathers in the day that I brought them up from the land of Egypt, even to this day, warning persistently, saying, "Listen to My voice."

8 'Yet they did not obey or incline their ear, but walked, each one, in the stubbornness of his evil heart; therefore I brought on them all the words of this covenant, which I commanded them to do, but they did not.' "

9 Then the LORD said to me, "A conspiracy has been found among the men of Judah and among the inhabitants of Jerusalem.

10 "They have turned back to the iniquities of their ancestors who refused to hear My words, and they have gone after other gods to serve them; the house of Israel and the house of Judah have broken My covenant which I made with their fathers."

11 Therefore thus says the LORD, "Behold I am bringing disaster on them which they will not be able to escape; though they will cry to Me, yet I will not listen to them."

JEREMIAH 31:31-34

31 "Behold, days are coming," declares the LORD, "when I will make a new covenant with the house of Israel and with the house of Judah,

32 not like the covenant which I made with their fathers in the day I took them by the hand to bring them out of the land of Egypt, My covenant which they broke, although I was a husband to them," declares the LORD.

33 "But this is the covenant which I will make with the house of Israel after those days," declares the LORD, "I will put My law within them and on their heart I will write it; and I will be their God, and they shall be My people.

34 "They will not teach again, each man his neighbor and each man his brother, saying, 'Know the LORD,' for they will all know Me, from the least of them to the greatest of them," declares the LORD, "for I will forgive their iniquity, and their sin I will remember no more."

GALATiANS 5:16-26

16 But I say, walk by the Spirit, and you will not carry out the desire of the flesh.

17 For the flesh sets its desire against the Spirit, and the Spirit against the flesh; for these are in opposition to one another, so that you may not do the things that you please.

18 But if you are led by the Spirit, you are not under the Law.

19 Now the deeds of the flesh are evident, which are: immorality, impurity, sensuality,

20 idolatry, sorcery, enmities, strife, jealousy, outbursts of anger, disputes, dissensions, factions,

21 envying, drunkenness, carousing, and things like these, of which I forewarn you, just as I have forewarned you, that those who practice such things will not inherit the kingdom of God.

22 But the fruit of the Spirit is love, joy, peace, patience, kindness, goodness, faithfulness,

23 gentleness, self-control; against such things there is no law.

24 Now those who belong to Christ Jesus have crucified the flesh with its passions and desires.

25 If we live by the Spirit, let us also walk by the Spirit.

26 Let us not become boastful, challenging one another, envying one another.

BRING THE WHOLE COUNSEL OF GOD'S WORD TO KIDS!

◀ GENESIS
God's Amazing Creation (Genesis 1–2)
Digging Up the Past (Genesis 3–11)
Abraham, God's Brave Explorer (Genesis 11–25)
Extreme Adventures with God (Genesis 24–36)
Joseph, God's Superhero (Genesis 37–50)

◀ DANIEL
You're a Brave Man, Daniel! (Daniel 1–6)
Fast-Forward to the Future (Daniel 7–12)

◀ JONAH
Wrong Way, Jonah!

◀ GOSPEL OF JOHN
Jesus in the Spotlight (John 1–10)
Jesus—Awesome Power, Awesome Love (John 11–16)
Jesus—To Eternity and Beyond (John 17–21)

◀ 2 TIMOTHY
Becoming God's Champion

◀ JAMES
Boy, Have I Got Problems!

◀ REVELATION
Bible Prophecy for Kids (Revelation 1–7)
A Sneak Peek into the Future (Revelation 8–22)

◀ TOPICAL & SKILLS
God, What's Your Name? (Names of God)
Lord, Teach Me to Pray for Kids
How to Study Your Bible for Kids (also available in DVD)
Cracking the Covenant Code for Kids

To find out about more
Discover 4 Yourself Bible Studies,
log on to our website:
www.HarvestHousePublishers.com